CHOCOLATE
NATIONS

ABOUT THE AUTHOR

Órla Ryan works for the *Financial Times* in London. She lived in Africa for four years, first in Uganda and then in Ghana, where she worked for Reuters.

CHOCOLATE
NATIONS

LIVING AND DYING
FOR COCOA
IN WEST AFRICA

ÓRLA RYAN

Zed Books

LONDON | NEW YORK

in association with

International African Institute
Royal African Society
Social Science Research Council

Chocolate Nations: Living and Dying for Cocoa in West Africa
was first published in association with
the International African Institute, the Royal African Society
and the Social Science Research Council in 2011 by
Zed Books Ltd, 7 Cynthia Street, London N1 9JF, UK
and Room 400, 175 Fifth Avenue, New York, NY 10010, USA

www.zedbooks.co.uk
www.internationalafricaninstitute.org
www.royalafricansociety.org
www.ssrc.org

Typeset in Monotype Bulmer by illuminati, Grosmont
Index by John Barker
Cover designed by Rogue Four Design
Printed and bound in the UK by CPI Anthony Rowe,
Chippenham and Eastbourne

Distributed in the USA exclusively by Palgrave Macmillan, a division of
St Martin's Press, LLC, 175 Fifth Avenue, New York, NY 10010, USA

A catalogue record for this book is available from the British Library
Library of Congress Cataloging in Publication Data available

ISBN 978 1 84813 004 3 hb
ISBN 978 1 84813 005 0 pb
ISBN 978 1 84813 540 6 eb

CONTENTS

ACKNOWLEDGEMENTS

I wish to thank the many people without whom it would have been very difficult, if not impossible, to complete this book. Thanks to Ali Basma for his help and insights into the Ghanaian cocoa market. I am truly sorry he is not here to read the finished manuscript. Also in Ghana, I wish to thank John Newman for making the time to talk about cocoa with me during and since my stay in West Africa. Others who helped in Ghana were Nana Amo Adade Boamah, Newman Ofosu, Kwasi Kpodo and Joseph Boateng in Kumasi. Thanks to Muhsin Barko for friendship and help in Accra and since. In Côte d'Ivoire, Yao Konan's help was invaluable. I also wish to thank Peter Murphy, Ange Aboa, Loucoumane Coulibaly and Charles Bamba for their help and advice in Abidjan and Bouake. Steve Wallace showed great patience with my questions, as did Jonathan Parkman. Thanks to Pascal Fletcher and Alistair Thomson, formerly in the Dakar bureau of Reuters, for funding my trips and accepting my stories. Also at Reuters, Eleanor Wason was very generous with her contacts and expertise. Thanks to Russell Miles, Karen Palmer, Sophie Hares, Emily Bowers and Blake Lambert for advice on the manuscript.

Richard Dowden and Stephanie Kitchen were encouraging and helpful throughout in spite of all my delays. I also wish to thank the Fund for Investigative Journalism for their financial support and advice. Thanks as ever to Mum, Dad, Oona, Fiona, Eoin and Sile. Most of all I want to thank those who took professional or personal risks to speak with me about the cocoa sector.

INTRODUCTION

The deep rich purple of the Cadbury chocolate bar is everywhere in Bournville, an English town with bowling clubs, a fairground and manicured green gardens. The bluey-violet shade is splashed on the railings at the train station, on street signs and park fences and, a short walk from the terminal, at the entrance to the chocolate factory. For millions of people, this colour conjures up the first bite of Dairy Milk, Crunchie or Creme Egg. These bars are the taste of childhood, and in this small town in the middle of Britain the Cadbury family has built one of the world's largest sweet companies.

I went to Bournville on a grey July day in 2009 and joined hundreds of people at Cadbury World, a theme park, where, the adverts say, chocolate comes to life. The exhibition begins with noisy parakeets and waterfalls in a Central American jungle, the source of cocoa, the main ingredient for chocolate, commonly believed to be an Aztec word derived from *xocolatl,* where *xococ* means sour and *atl* water. On display are tiny models of the European explorers who in the sixteenth and seventeenth centuries took the dried brown beans to their home countries. In the nineteenth century, the Cadbury brothers began to experiment with cocoa in their tea store in Bull Street in Birmingham. In 1879, they built a factory in a town they named Bournville and in the years that followed they started to make milk chocolate.

As the tour progresses, parents and grandparents jostle with buggies and fidgety children. Clammy hands grip complimentary bars and hungry eyes watch workers cut chocolate models from plastic moulds. A small boy in a white shirt presses his face against the glass, entranced by the never-ending stream of bars chugging along a conveyor belt in the packaging factory. Elsewhere, a television screen plays Cadbury advertisements on a loop.

For these visitors, the exhibition offers not just handfuls of treats but also a glimpse into British social history. On display are the first tins of drinking cocoa and bars of chocolate, as well as the vast array of sweets sold today. For more than a hundred years, Cadbury drinking cocoa and eating chocolate have been part of British life.

The beans that flavour this chocolate come from Ghana. Cocoa may have originated in the Americas but the global centre of production is now West Africa. African farmers produce the basic ingredient for Creme Eggs, Dairy Milk and Fruit and Nut, all the bars stacked high at train station kiosks, corner shops and supermarkets. Without them, this whole business would crumble.

Yet the role played by African producers is surprisingly little known. Cadbury centred its 2009 advertising campaign around its links with Ghana. Yet it scarcely features in the Cadbury World exhibition. The common view of the global cocoa map is seriously skewed. When I told people in the UK I was writing about the trade, most voiced surprise at the fact that so many beans came from West Africa. In their minds, they linked cocoa with South America. Yet more than 50 per cent of the world's beans come from Ghana, the world's second-biggest producer, and its neighbour Côte d'Ivoire, the world's biggest. Nearly 2 million small producers in West Africa, including those in Cameroon and Nigeria, produced 2.3 million tonnes in 2008–09, accounting for roughly two-thirds of the total world crop of 3.5 million tonnes.[1]

I know about cocoa because I lived in Ghana for two years until the end of 2007. I went there as a journalist, hired by Reuters to cover the country and its cocoa trade for its general and financial news service. Before I went I spent some weeks in the London office covering commodities. This involved speaking to traders about market movements and writing daily reports. What I found in Ghana was so different as to be shocking. This trade was more than just numbers flickering on a computer screen; it involved flesh-and-blood lives. There are 64 kilos of beans in a bag and sixteen bags to a tonne. Hundreds of thousands of farmers work to produce 650,000 tonnes or so of cocoa a year. It is a huge, nationwide physical effort to gather these beans and to truck them out on potholed roads to the port. This was gross domestic product broken down into man, woman and child hours. This was a real-life lesson in economics. The hundreds of millions of dollars earned every year from their sale kept the nation ticking over. For the first time I felt I understood what it meant to describe a product as the lifeblood of a country. I felt physically as far away from the commodity exchange in London as I could possibly be, yet what happened in Ghana and Côte d'Ivoire was inextricably linked with what happened in the City of London and in factories such as the one at Bournville.

I had to follow the cocoa market in unusual depth. Or at least a level of depth that was unusual for a journalist. While talking to people about politics, religion and just life in general helped me understand Ghana, I felt that writing about how the industry worked, how farmers were treated and their relationship with companies like Cadbury provided me with an inside track on what the country was really like. I could see how the Marketing Board rewarded the government's friends, how buyers curried favour with the regulator and how producers struggled to get by. I travelled to Côte d'Ivoire and saw how battles over land and identity had sullied the reputation of a nation once seen as a miracle state. The production of these beans is written into the economic and political history of Ghana and Côte d'Ivoire. Deciphering their cocoa economies helped me to learn a bit more not only about them but also about their relationships with the world's richer countries.

When I visited villages in Ghana, I found that producers left fresh beans to dry on reed trays outside their homes. As the beans fermented, a rich chocolatey perfume and taste developed. This was a smell both familiar and foreign to me, an intense aroma which conjured up childhood images of Flakes, Milk Tray selections and Mars bars. But the scent that reminded me of childhood treats meant different things to these farmers. A good crop meant they had money to spare. A bad one meant poverty. These were beans they lived and died for. This was the hard economic end of my everyday luxury. This was not just the other side of the world from Bournville but also the other side of the story.

The taste of chocolate mattered little to these producers. Most had never bitten into a bar. This is in sharp contrast to South America, where chocolate is infused with a rich cultural and mystical significance. The Aztecs had used the beans as a currency and enjoyed a bitter cocoa drink laced with chilli. They believed cocoa possessed spiritual or even magical qualities. Cocoa became known as the Food of the Gods.

In West Africa, cocoa and chocolate do not feature in local recipes or ceremonies. The tree is not native to the region. It is a relative newcomer, arriving in the former British colony almost

by accident. Local legend has it that Tetteh Quarshie, a migrant
farm labourer, brought the first pod to his native land in 1879
from Fernando Po, a tiny African island where Portuguese missionaries had brought the beans from Brazil. In the 1860s, Swiss
missionaries had experimented with seedlings from Surinam.[2]
There aren't many places in the world where the conditions are
right for cocoa. These trees like rainfall, shade and humidity,
flourishing in temperatures of 20°C to 32°C. They are fragile and
can take up to five years to bear fruit. But the climate and soil
in West Africa suited the crop. By 1887, the government was dis-
tributing seedlings in the Akwapim district.[3] Producers planted
them in plots not more than a few hectares in size. Unlike many
of the other products you find on supermarket shelves, cocoa is
and always has been a smallholder crop.

It seems amazing now, but in those early days there was little
awareness of cocoa's economic potential. Those planting cocoa
were also testing other crops. A report analysing agricultural opportunities in the Gold Coast only mentioned cocoa in passing.[4] In
the late nineteenth century, few sensed how important chocolate,
and cocoa, would become. The first chocolate bars were dry and
flaky. It seemed unlikely that demand for these strange sweets
would take off. But experiments in Bournville and elsewhere in
Europe helped shape demand for cocoa and chocolate. As manufacturers mastered their art and the technology advanced, they
became smooth and creamy. Initially, Cadbury imported cocoa
beans from São Tomé and Príncipe in Portuguese West Africa. But
newspaper reports of slavery encouraged it to look elsewhere.[5] It
shipped its first beans from what was then called the Gold Coast
in 1908.[6] From then on, the taste of Cadbury chocolate would be
the taste of Ghanaian cocoa.

I made regular trips to cocoa farms for Reuters. It quickly
became clear that smallholders wanted a better life than cocoa

had given them. I was struck by the fact that many did not want their children to farm the crop. They wanted them to become doctors, lawyers and teachers. They wanted their horizons to extend beyond the next harvest. At the same time, the contrast between these simple gatherings of mud dwellings and multi-national profits was stark. While the global market for chocolate and cocoa products is worth $75 billion a year,[7] Ghana's cocoa exports were worth $1.2 billion in 2008.[8] This is one of the country's biggest exports. It is an essential ingredient for one of the world's most popular sweets. Yet cocoa farmers receive just 4 per cent of the final price of an average UK bar of milk chocolate.[9]

For decades, these beans have fed Western factories, eager to fill demand for chocolate which for the past thirty years has risen in line with global GDP, a climb likely to continue in the years ahead. Cocoa output has nearly tripled since the 1960s.[10] Much of this extra production has come from West Africa. But for the past three years, demand for beans has outstripped supply.[11] Industry can no longer assume there will be enough cocoa to satiate our appetite for chocolate. The trees are old and farmers are disgruntled with their lot. When I spoke to industry officials, they talked about the need to encourage smallholders to stick with cocoa. They voiced fears about where they would get their beans from in the future. Some, not all, looked again at producers' lives and wondered how they could earn more from the beans. Increasingly, people talked about sustainability, the need to ensure smallholders made enough not just to live but also to invest in the crop and their future.

I started to write this book because I wanted to convey how important cocoa was to these countries and to understand why they seemed to have earned so little from it. It is based on the hundreds of conversations and interviews I had about cocoa during my time in West Africa and since I left. In many ways, it is about power and how it is wielded by supermarkets, manufacturers and, most importantly, governments. It looks at why farmers lack a voice at home and why producing countries lack one globally. What emerges is that smallholders need political leadership and negotiating muscle. At the same time, producers need education, scientific support and land reform. Chocolate companies need to be more transparent about their dealings in the region. Fairtrade, the most frequently touted solution to farmer poverty, is in itself not an answer. There is no one bar of chocolate you can buy which will resolve the situations that I describe in this book. But everything points to the fact that if producers are to enjoy a better standard of living, chocolate lovers will have to get used to paying more for their favourite treat.

As I walked around the Cadbury exhibition, listening to advertising jingles and watching bars roll by on the packaging line, I wondered if it mattered that few people knew where cocoa came from. The images at Bournville jarred with life lived on Ghanaian farms and villages, where producers lack running water and electricity and live in simple dwellings. I wondered if the contrast between this well-kept town in central England and the poverty of African farmers was simply too shocking to convey on a family day out. But I left Bournville thinking an opportunity had been missed. Food colours our understanding of different parts of the world and of how cultures and economies knit together. It can fill in the gaps left by more conventional histories. The families leaving Cadbury World have only half the story. There is a much bigger tale to tell about chocolate.

ONE

GHANA IS COCOA

On the shoulders of peasant farmers

The smell of cocoa, rich and sweet, is in the air in Larwehkrom, a village in western Ghana. Small brown beans dry on reed trays. Nearby trees are overgrown and heavy with green pods, large and small. In the weeks and months to come, these oval husks will ripen into yellow. Farmers will crack their hard shells and empty them of their white pulpy seeds, which they will sift, sort and dry. But now it is July, a low point in the season. The settlement is quiet. Skies are overcast. Children play with old bicycle tyres. Goats scrabble in the dirt near a stack of silvery tin basins. A kettle rumbles on a charcoal stove and a battery radio rattles out the news. Rain patters on the tin roof of his mud-brick house as Samuel Tei Larweh, 63, a village leader and an elder in the Church of Pentecost, sits on a wooden bench.[1]

Larweh first came to this part of the country, then called the Gold Coast, at the age of 11. He left his home in the east to join his father, a timber contractor, in the west. Here, temperatures are high, rain falls in abundance and crops flourish in the rich and fertile soil. At that time, demand was growing for cocoa, the key ingredient in what was becoming the world's favourite sweet, chocolate. In 1959, with few trees left to fell, his father, Stephen Tetteh Larweh, decided to become a farmer.

Samuel's father was part of a long tradition of restless, pioneering cocoa farmers. These producers began growing the crop in the country's east in the late nineteenth century. They planted locally and then moved in search of new land to expand their farms. They paid in cash or shared the harvest with the local chief and labourers. With the money they made, they built new houses in their home towns and educated their children. As they expanded, cocoa swept from east to west. Eventually, it arrived in the district of Sefwi Wiawso, the westernmost part of Ghana, which its inhabitants now call the country's cocoa capital. Hundreds of people settled at the bottom of the hill in a village named Larwehkrom, after Stephen, its first farmer. Cocoa became known as the profitable tree. As the lyrics of one song popular in the 1950s put it:

> If you want to send your children to school, it is cocoa
> If you want to build your house, it is cocoa
> If you want to marry, it is cocoa
> If you want to buy cloth, it is cocoa
> If you want to buy lorry, it is cocoa
> Whatever you want to do in this world
> It is with cocoa money that you do it.

These small producers contributed to an explosion in global output. In 1895, world exports totalled 77,000 metric tonnes, with most of this cocoa coming from South America and the Caribbean.[2] By 1925, exports reached more than 500,000 tonnes and the Gold Coast had become a leading exporter of cocoa, feeding chocolate factories all around the world. This increase was extraordinary, not least because this was not and has never been a plantation crop. Right from the start, these beans came mainly from small farms, most not more than a couple of acres in size.

The cocoa boom, wrote William Nowell, a senior British civil servant, was 'spontaneous and irresistible, almost unregulated'.[3] In a government report in 1938, he wrote:

> We found in the Gold Coast an agricultural industry that perhaps has no parallel in the world. Within about forty years, cocoa farming has developed from nothing until it now occupies a dominant position in the country's economy – cocoa being virtually the only commercial crop – and provides two fifths of the world's requirements. Yet the industry began and remains in the hands of small, independent native farmers.[4]

The output of these smallholders has shaped not only the chocolate business but also the country itself. In those early heady days of the boom, new roads were constructed to help people get the beans out of the village and to the port. Buyers opened depots and wealthier producers built double-storeyed houses.[5] Farmers frequently owned multiple plantations and absentee landlords were common.[6] Politicians joke that it was a mistake for the colonialists to call the country the Gold Coast because, although it has gold, this is a nation, everyone agrees, built from cocoa money. As the saying goes, 'Cocoa is Ghana and Ghana is Cocoa'.

These beans have helped Larweh to feed and educate his children and enabled him to build a new house in his home town. Larweh seemed to me hardworking and resourceful. He grew other crops as well as cocoa, and people in the village spoke highly of him. But when I looked around the settlement in which he lived, he seemed to have little to show for his hard work. Larweh, his hair speckled with grey, has torch and lamplight, not electricity. A new borehole means the villagers now have clean water, but the village still lacks a school. A closer look at their relationships with buyers and government since independence offers an insight into why smallholders have remained so poor. Over the past fifty years, farmers have been at the mercy of the price the government has decided to pay them.

Fight for independence

Not far from the sea in Accra, a massive grey stone monument rises like the base of a tree hacked off in its prime. This is a tribute to Kwame Nkrumah, the country's first president. This neatly kept park provides a brief respite from the hawkers and traffic jams of the nearby high street. The thunder of the sea is faintly audible and the gardens are usually empty. I went to the memorial with a visitor from London in 2007. She knew little about Ghana until I moved there. This is not that surprising. Ghana is peaceful and quiet and rarely makes headlines in British newspapers. But a generation earlier, the Gold Coast was one of Britain's best-known colonies. More than fifty years ago, the events in this quiet park, once the old British polo grounds, made front-page news the world over. On 6 March 1957, Nkrumah declared it free of colonial control and named it Ghana. This was the first country in sub-Saharan Africa to gain independence. What happened in this part of West Africa made news editors sit up.

Ghana's independence heralded change, not just in Accra but across the continent. Inside the park on that day in March 1957 were the Duchess of Kent, representing the British Queen; Richard Nixon, then vice president of the USA; Martin Luther King; and Wilbur de Paris, the American jazz musician.[7] A lot rested on Ghana's success, a leader in *The Times* of London noted.

> Dr Nkrumah's life speaks for the fact that it is his mission to win independence, not only for Ghana, but for the rest of Africa as well ... The surest way of fulfilling it is by making Ghana a prosperous,

reliable and democratic state. That will destroy at one blow both the hesitation of honest doubters and the arguments of those who seek to prolong domination for their own selfish motives.[8]

Hopes were high. Thanks to the hard work of its peasant producers, the new country had money in the bank.[9] 'The world's passion for chocolate in the last decade brought a windfall which ... has given the country solid assets with very little indebtedness', a leader in the *Guardian* said.[10] The country owed a lot to its cocoa farmers, everyone seemed to agree. 'The man whose independence we are principally celebrating is the Ghana cocoa farmer', wrote Polly Hill, an academic, in the same newspaper.[11]

In the years that followed, Nkrumah was to become one of the best-known leaders in the world. Many in Ghana still voice pride in him. He secured the nation independence and a leading voice in politics across the continent. But this pride coexists with another reality. Ghana's first leader set the country on a road which impoverished its people, including its cocoa farmers.

Born in the country's west, Nkrumah had studied in the USA and Britain, where he attended Communist Party meetings. He returned home in late 1947,[12] determined to campaign for independence. His fiery rhetoric quickly attracted followers. Many of his admirers were 'verandah boys', youths who slept on the porches of rich men's houses because they had no homes of their own. His movement quickly gained momentum. Arrested and jailed for sedition after organising a general strike, he was released when the Convention People's Party (CPP), his political party, swept to victory in a 1951 election. Within twenty-four hours of his release from prison, Nkrumah was brought into government.[13]

But cocoa farmers were suspicious of Nkrumah. From the start, they had got a raw deal from buyers. In the early start of the twentieth century, they sold their beans to large exporters such as Cadbury or the United Africa Company, the biggest shipper. Producers felt they were being cheated. They believed scales were fixed to register a much lighter weight.[14] When, in 1937, the biggest purchasers decided to fix the farm-gate prices, planters refused to sell their beans or buy imported goods. After an eight-month boycott, the government, fearing unrest, decided to set up a marketing board.[15] From 1947, the Ghana Cocoa Board, or Cocobod, the country's marketing board, fixed the farm-gate price and dealt with multinational buyers on behalf of smallholders. Organisations similar to this already existed in Australia and New Zealand. They were seen as a way to increase producer bargaining power on the world market. But the creation of the Board also meant that their political leaders had easy access to cocoa funds. Farmers, burnt by their dealings with buyers, were wary.

Nkrumah made clear that cocoa revenues were central to his plans. 'Cocoa was and still is the mainstay of our economy. It accounted for 68 per cent of our exports in 1955', he wrote later in his autobiography. 'It belongs to the country and it affects everyone so we had to think of the general public as well as the cocoa farmers.' He added: 'By using cocoa funds for development and for providing amenities, it would be possible to improve the general standard of living in the country as a whole at an early date.'[16] As prime minister, Nkrumah asked the marketing board to fix farmer prices for four years from 1954,[17] even though international prices were rising. Cocoa farmers' worst fears about the new president appeared to be confirmed.

Battles over cocoa money almost derailed the path to independence. At that time, roughly half of the country's beans[18] were produced in the Ashanti region. Farmers feared that Ashanti interests were being overlooked by a nationalist movement whose leaders were from other parts of the country.[19] The National Liberation Movement wanted a federal government, one that gave a greater share of cocoa wealth to the regions that produced it. In elections in 1956, the NLM used a cocoa tree as its party symbol. It highlighted the widespread allegations of corruption at the marketing board.[20] 'What you need is an honest government,' one of its leaders said; 'one whose hand is not always in the public pocket.' Its manifesto outlined why farmers 'should vote for cocoa' and told farmers 'it is your money they want'. Nkrumah argued that those 'madmen who talk to you of cocoa and corruption' simply hide the fact 'that they do not want independence for our country'.

Nkrumah won the election and Ghana its independence. His plans to industrialise the country hinged on revenues from bean sales. The government-controlled marketing board set the price and it was easy for it to increase taxes. By 1965, farmers were paying £59 tax per tonne, 50 per cent more than they had paid in 1956.[21] These extra taxes financed Nkrumah's erratic spending and pet projects. He ordered an $18 million frigate from a British shipyard as a private command ship,[22] spent about $8 million on cocoa silos, ignoring advice that they were unsuitable,[23] and frittered nearly $50 million on a meeting for African leaders in Accra.[24] More than sixty embassies were opened abroad.[25] As farmer incomes fell, party members and government officials were increasingly well rewarded. In 1961, the president sought to stem party corruption. The imposed restrictions hinted at party members' wealth, noted Dennis Austin.[26] They were not allowed to own more than two houses with a combined value of £20,000 or possess more than two cars.

Nkrumah became increasingly reclusive and paranoid. He passed laws allowing him to jail people without trial and declared Ghana a one-party state.[27] He became president for life. Statues of the Messiah, as he was called, were put up around the country. His face adorned stamps and coins. Schoolchildren started their day, praising their leader.[28] Outside of Ghana, the international media, once excited about his regime, called him a spendthrift dictator.[29] At the same time, Nkrumah forged relationships with left-wing leaders around the world. The early 1960s were the height of the Cold War. President John F. Kennedy was president of the USA and Nikita Khruschchev was president of the Soviet Union. In 1959, Fidel Castro had assumed power in Cuba, aligning it with the Soviet Union. In this context, Nkrumah's friendship with Russia and China and his talk of an African socialism rattled the US and British governments.

The dollars earned from cocoa exports held the country together. In 1965, oversupply sent prices tumbling on the world market. Nkrumah blamed imperialists and neocolonialists for forcing prices lower.[30] Factories in Accra closed for lack of raw materials. Queues of shoppers formed in the streets for butter, milk, rice, sugar, salt and drugs.[31] In February 1966, when Nkrumah was on an official trip to China, he was overthrown in a coup, widely believed to have been backed by the USA and UK. On national radio, the coup-makers declared that the 'myth surrounding Kwame Nkrumah has been broken'. At independence, the country had reserves of $560 million. By 1966, they had long evaporated. Ghana had once been debt-free. By the time of Nkrumah's departure, its foreign debt totalled $1 billion,[32] much of it in short-term loans. On news of the coup, Ghanaians danced in the street.

A lifeline under revolutionary rule

Hawkers dart between cars on Accra's dual carriageways. They offer drivers everything from inflatable toilet seats to matches, their job made marginally less dangerous by the slow movement of traffic. Some sell posters, snaps of the latest Nigerian movie star, a map of Africa or a picture of Michael Essien, the Chelsea midfielder. Frequently, the picture they unroll is of an unsmiling man with sharp cheekbones in military uniform and dark sunglasses. This is Flight Lieutenant Jerry John Rawlings, who led Ghana for nearly twenty years. When he first took power in a coup in 1979, farmers were earning a pittance. But by the end of his rule, their lives and earnings had begun to improve.

The first Ghanaians heard of Jerry Rawlings was on 15 May 1979.[33] Life in the capital was close to breaking point. Shortages were rampant. Operations had been suspended at Korle-bu, Accra's main hospital, as supplies had run out. That day, office workers stayed at home after reports of gunshots at the military headquarters. They feared the army was about to take to the streets. By midday, news had filtered out that an uprising by a gangly 25-year-old airman had been quelled.

At a general court martial later that month, Rawlings complained of corruption. He called for bloodshed to 'clean the country'.[34] His supporters feared that the charismatic airman would be executed, but Rawlings acted quickly. On the morning of 4 June, those who tuned into the six o clock broadcast on Radio Ghana heard Rawlings's distinctive voice for the first time. The government had been overthrown, he said. The Armed Forces Revolutionary Council had taken control of Ghana.[35]

The new regime proved to be brutal. Three former presidents were executed and several military commanders were killed. Harsh treatment was meted out to those guilty of 'economic crimes'. These were broadly defined. A person who hoarded goods or charged high prices could be found guilty. So could someone who owned a second car, had a professional job or owned two houses. Soldiers were quick to pass judgement on anyone who appeared to have money. 'You could not even explain to some of the young soldiers that you borrowed money from a bank; for them borrowing money from a bank meant someone was doing you a favour', Kwame Pianim, head of the Cocoa marketing board at the time of the coup, told me. In August that year, officers dynamited Makola market, reducing it to rubble as punishment to the market women. The so-called 'Makola mummies' had refused to lower their prices,[36] one of the most serious economic crimes.

The cocoa marketing board's executives also attracted attention. They were known for their big houses, cars and large drinks allowances. 'It seemed strange to many people that officials at the CMB should be enjoying more out of whatever money that comes from cocoa than the farmers who did the work', wrote an editorial in the *Daily Graphic*, one of the country's main newspapers.[37] Nobody monitored what these officials spent, said Pianim, who tried to tighten spending and controls at the Board. If an auditor had visited the marketing board, he said, he would have found nothing to audit. Under pressure from the new government to account for their spending, cocoa bureaucrats fled in fear of their lives.

This clampdown on corruption was dubbed a 'house cleaning' exercise. But Rawlings had no economic or political strategy to speak of. He stepped down in September to make way for a new government. He then staged a second coup the following year. The former airman clearly saw himself as a revolutionary. He praised Fidel Castro, the communist president of Cuba, and Muammar Gaddafi, the Libyan president. In the booming voice that prompted some of his followers to call him Junior Jesus, he said: 'Don't ask me what my ideology or economic programme is. I don't know any law and I don't understand economics, but I know it when my stomach is empty.'[38]

But while Rawlings boasted about his ignorance of economics, he knew exactly how important cocoa was to Ghana. The crop was its main source of foreign currency, exchanged not just for dollars but also for basic goods, such as sugar from Cuba and tyres and chemicals from the then East Germany.[39] Without cocoa the country would have ground to a halt, yet farmers received little. The cedi was overvalued and inflation was so high that 'whatever you paid the farmers wasn't enough', Pianim said. Increasingly, smallholders were sending their harvest to Côte d'Ivoire, where prices were higher. 'If my mother or father were a cocoa farmer, I would smuggle too', Rawlings told Pianim. The advantage of a dictatorship, said Pianim wryly, is that decisions can be made very quickly.

> Nobody was interested [in raising farmer prices] because for the government this was an easy source of tax revenue. But when the coup took place, in one of my first meetings with Rawlings, I asked for a price increase. He said what is the price now, I explained it to him. In 15 minutes, I had gotten a price adjustment for cocoa, which I had been trying for six months to get and which had proven difficult to be able to get. The only way you can make farmers do their work and be able to earn foreign exchange for the country was to increase the price. Of course he understood what he was doing.

This meagre price rise failed to stop the smuggling of cocoa to nearby Côte d'Ivoire. By 1983, Ghana was producing just 160,000 tonnes of cocoa a year, down from more than 500,000 tonnes in 1965,[40] and it had lost its title as the world's biggest grower to its neighbour. For many smallholders, there was little incentive to grow the crop. Cadbury, which had built the taste of its chocolate on Ghanaian beans, was 'genuinely scared', one former executive said. 'Where the hell were we going to get it from?' he asked.

Life was tough and not just for cocoa farmers. Store shelves were empty and imported goods were scarce. People spent days looking for food. One lawyer living in Accra at the time provided a vivid example of what it was like to live under such shortages:

> You get up in the morning, you have only a tin of milk and you have children and you know this tin of milk will get finished by

tomorrow morning, so you will spend time which you would have spent in office to do work to go and look for the manager [to buy milk], who because of pressure on him [to source goods] might also have gone to hide.

As businessmen left and factories shut down, well-off Accra dwellers drove to the countryside at weekends looking for food. Even now in Ghana, those who do not have enough to eat, whose bones jut out around their neck, are said to be wearing the Rawlings chain. By the early 1980s, the government's revolutionary rhetoric had begun to soften. Rawlings asked Paul Victor Obeng, a friend of his wife, to join his government. Obeng warned the president that people could turn against him if life didn't get better. He told him: 'You say openly you came for the ordinary people and if the ordinary people themselves are now becoming victims of these brutalities, they will find it difficult to realise that you are here for them.'

Ghana needed cash. For Obeng, it was clear that cocoa could provide a route out of the morass. 'It dawned on us that we should salvage the economy by salvaging our crops and goods that would be convertible into foreign exchange. Cocoa was the major one and it was the easiest', he said. Some farmers sent their cocoa to Côte d'Ivoire, but most had little choice but to sell it to the government. Obeng, who became minister for cocoa, said: 'If cocoa had been maize, they may have eaten it, they may have decided to feed it to chickens [but] the internal usage of cocoa is limited, they had to surrender and sell.' To encourage farmers to grow more cocoa, the government began to increase prices.

These changes in Ghana came at a time of global upheaval. The Cold War was ending. President Reagan was in power in America and Mrs Thatcher led Britain. The socialist policies that Rawlings had adhered to had lost credibility not just at home, but elsewhere around the world. The Washington Consensus, a set of standard policy prescriptions for developing countries, had emerged. The decline of the Soviet Union was clearly a turning point for Ghana, one observer said. To this day, it is not unusual to meet Ghanaians who have worked or been educated in the Soviet Union or countries aligned to it. With the decline of Communism, he said, 'Rawlings was smart enough to change sides very quickly. Think of how many Ghanaians you met [who were] educated in Moscow. They were very fast to change.'

Western donors began to offer money to countries interested in introducing free-market reforms. The Rawlings regime quickly signed up. These policies brought painful change. Tens of thousands of public servants were sacked,[41] state enterprises began to be privatised and a slow devaluation of the cedi began. Inflation fell, and the economy began to grow. By 1995, the Cocoa Board employed roughly one-tenth of the 100,000 people it had employed a decade earlier. Farmers, newly motivated by rising prices, began to plant cocoa. Production began to rise.

The first time I met Rawlings it was a few weeks before the fiftieth anniversary of Ghana's independence in 2007. The Golden Jubilee was to be celebrated by street parties, a national holiday and a fortnight's break from the power cuts that left the country without electricity half the time. By then, he had been out of power for nearly eight years. He had left in 2000 to make way for John Kufuor, his democratically elected successor. In person, Rawlings is a far cry from the dashing lieutenant of the posters. He has a paunch, wears glasses and his hair is streaked with grey.

Rawlings still divides Ghana. P.V. Obeng describes him as a man angry at the 'sea of corruption' in the country. Kwame Pianim, later imprisoned by Rawlings for an alleged coup attempt, says that when he first took power he was 'humane, he was understanding, he listened … He was also for justice, if he thought something was unfair, he said it was unfair.' But

Rawlings changed into a 'completely different' person after the second coup, he said. These were fearful times, he said, 'very very frightening'. For many, the man who talks of River Gods and voodoo is uneducated and brutal. In his early days, one reporter from the time told me, he was simply a good-looking frontman for army militants.

Rawlings continues to make headlines in the local press. In tribute to his distinctive voice and his reputation as a coup-maker, the word 'boom' is street slang for a *coup d'état*. He also retains many loyal followers. The driver who accompanied me to the interview was clearly starstruck and wanted his picture taken with the former president. A large figure with a big voice, Rawlings, now over 60, was intimidating but also eager to get it right. He brought out different patterned shirts and asked me which one would look best on television. His voice still booms, though he is often rambling and incoherent. That day, he was angry that a close friend had been jailed for corruption. He feared the current government had a vendetta against members of his regime. It was frequently difficult to understand the point he was trying to make. The water in his toilet cistern, he told me, was better than what most Ghanaians were drinking. Ghana has many problems, said Rawlings, but he has no regrets from his time in power.

No simple success story

In 2002, the Irish rock singer Bono visited Makola market in central Accra, with Paul O Neill, the then US Treasury secretary. He posed with market traders, their stalls stacked high with fabric, food and second-hand clothes. He later chatted to schoolchildren and held meetings with President Kufuor. For an anti-poverty crusader, Ghana is a good destination. It held its first democratic elections in 1992 and since then has had two changes of power. Rawlings made way for John Kufuor and his New Patriotic Party in 2000, and John Atta Mills, vice president under Rawlings, took office after closely contested elections in late 2008. Ghana enjoys stability and steady economic growth. It earns money from cocoa, gold and timber. It will soon have oil. It had gross national income per capita of $691 in 2008,[42] and its economy is forecast to continue growing at about 5 per cent.[43] It is better off than many countries in sub-Saharan Africa.

This story of relative success is more complicated than it at first appears. Many still endure power cuts and water shortages. Wealth is concentrated in the capital, where thousands flock in search of work. Infant and child mortality rates in the north are among the region's highest. President Kufuor's government was seen to favour people from the Ashanti region, just as Rawlings's administration rewarded those in the East, the Ewe. Drug trafficking increased. After Kufuor's departure, several corruption scandals emerged. Every year, hundreds of Ghanaians, desperate for a fresh start, head overland to Senegal or Libya. There they attempt a dangerous trip by small boat to Europe. The economy has made impressive gains since the 1970s, yet a simple label of success fails to convey fully the reality of living in Ghana. But cocoa farmers have enjoyed one dividend of democracy: farm-gate prices have risen steadily.

Under pressure from the International Monetary Fund and the World Bank, the Rawlings administration committed to increasing producer prices. Since then, successive governments have promised to pay smallholders at least 70 per cent of the sale price it receives for cocoa.[44] It frequently misses this target. It is not unusual for farmers to receive just 50 per cent of the world market price. This partly reflects the nature of the advance sale system (discussed in Chapter 7) and the government's continued reliance on cocoa. But the price paid to farmers continues to rise. The government faces strong electoral pressure to reward farmers. The country's 720,000 producers and their dependants make up roughly one-quarter of the Ghanaian population of just over 20 million people. No political party would mess with a voting bloc this size. It is genuinely hard to imagine that any administration, of any political hue, could, as the military regime did in 1977, pay farmers £347 a tonne at a time when world prices were in excess of £3,000.[45] As one industry executive told me, it is now seen as politically impossible actually to reduce the farm-gate price. As prices have increased, so has production. The harvest now averages about 650,000 tonnes a year, reaching just over 710,000 tonnes in 2008-09.[46] Ghana provides roughly 20 per cent of the global crop. Farmers have a history of being cheated by government and buyers, but democracy helps to keep government on its toes.

Yet smallholders remain poor. The disparity between Ghana's rural poverty and urban wealth remains as clear today as it was when Nowell wrote in 1938 that 'the wealth of the country is reflected in its excellent roads, in its schools at Achimota and elsewhere and in the scale and style of the Government buildings in Accra; less so in the appearance of the provincial towns; and least of all in the amenities of the country villages.'

Even with rising prices, a rural household's income from cocoa rarely exceeds a few dollars a day.[47] Plots are small and yields are low. Producers struggle to invest in their farms. Many cannot afford fertiliser. Larweh doubts his children will till the land themselves. The farmer's life remains hard, precarious, reliant on wind and rain and sunshine and a price that someone else decides. This is not a job to which the upwardly mobile aspire. This industry was built on the shoulders of peasant farmers. Yet they have little to show for it. As I left Larwehkrom, I wondered what else needed to happen before producers could truly profit from their harvest.

TWO

COCOA WARS

A missing man

In a small town in Côte d'Ivoire, the world's biggest producer
of cocoa, Thomas Coulibaly[1] is searching for his father. It is
November 2006, the peak of the cocoa season and a busy time
of year in Duékoué. This is when farmers spend long days on
the farm, eager to cut down the ripe pods, harvest their beans
and sell them as quickly as they can. This is when producers
earn the money they need to survive for the rest of the year. But,
unlike in Ghana, tensions rise during this busy harvest period.
While people with land have money, those without have little.
Immigrants prosper and local people become angry. This anger
can turn to violence.

Thomas and his family come from the north of the country
and have lived in Duékoué in the country's south-west for more
than thirty years. But they are still viewed as outsiders. That day,
Thomas's father, a cocoa and coffee farmer who lived with his
family in the town, said he wanted to go to the farm. Thomas
knew that immigrants had been murdered on their plantations
and he feared for his father's safety. He pleaded with him to stay

at home. But his father promised to take care and to return early. Now, only a day since he saw him, Thomas fears he will never see him again.

The cocoa and coffee grown around towns such as Duékoué is the pivot on which the Ivorian economy turns. Cocoa alone is one of the nation's biggest export earners, supporting nearly half of its population. About 200,000 tonnes of these beans are harvested in this western part of the country[2] every year, roughly 15 per cent of the annual Ivorian output of 1.2 million tonnes.[3]

This cocoa is also a vital part of world market supply. Roughly one-third[4] of the world's produce comes from Côte d'Ivoire. The ubiquity of Ivorian beans is such that unless a bar of chocolate explicitly states its ingredients originated elsewhere, nearly every bar you buy will contain at least some from its plantations. This cocoa flavours cappucinos, cakes and chocolate bars the world over. As the story of Thomas's father makes clear, some of these beans are soaked in blood.

Miracle state

Thomas and his family are from a small town called Tieko in the region of Odienne, the north-west of Côte d'Ivoire. They came to Duékoué in 1976 in search of fertile land to till. Sidibe, Thomas's father, bought 5 hectares for nearly $700. Half the land was already planted with coffee and he planted cocoa. His family of ten thrived. Life was sweet, Thomas says. They had their own house. In school holidays, he worked on the plantation. His father could 'feed his children without begging' and he could send them to school.

The story of the family's journey to Duékoué begins some sixteen years before their arrival in the town. It starts in 1960 when Côte d'Ivoire won its independence from France and

Felix Houphouet Boigny became the independent country's first president. Unlike Kwame Nkrumah, the leader of neighbouring Ghana, Boigny did not favour industrialisation. If Côte d'Ivoire is to prosper, the Ivorian president said, farmers should grow coffee and cocoa. He welcomed immigrants with open arms and he made land freely available to those who wanted to work it. In these two decisions lie the secrets of the success of the Ivorian cocoa industry and the roots of its downfall.

Under President Boigny, those who cut down the forest trees, dug up the soil and planted cocoa could claim ownership of the land. Hundreds of thousands of people came in search of land to till. Some came from Boigny's own ethnic group, the Baoule. Others came from northern Côte d'Ivoire. Many more arrived from Burkina Faso and Mali, the landlocked countries to the Ivorian north. They struck deals for land with local people, known as their *tuteurs*.[5] Côte d'Ivoire welcomed these immigrants. Its national anthem saluted this *pays de l'hospitalité*. Cocoa farming took off in Côte d'Ivoire.

Boigny's policies on land and immigration echoed those of the colonialists. Under French rule, boundaries had been fluid. During the 1930s, the French brought together large chunks of Haute Volta, now known as Burkina Faso, and parts of northern Côte d'Ivoire.[6] In the years that followed, borders shifted again. Ivorian identity and borders seemed to be in a perpetual state of flux. It became common for people in the south to perceive the Dioula of the north, who were often Muslim, as foreigners.

While the Europeans had brought cocoa to Côte d'Ivoire, African smallholders were responsible for the explosion in output. At first they struggled to get workers, as French planters were able to conscript workers from any village in the country. Boigny, a well-to-do farmer and doctor, campaigned to end the forced labour system. With its abolition on 3 April 1946, he earned the support of the country's farmers, now able to staff their cocoa plantations. Boigny became a major, almost mythical, figure in Ivorian politics.

When Côte d'Ivoire won its independence in 1960, Boigny quickly stood out from other leaders across the continent. He had served in French governments and was close friends with many politicians there. He was happy to turn to France for aid and economic advice. Encouraged by the French-backed CFA franc, French businessmen invested heavily in Côte d'Ivoire, its French population rising from 10,000 in 1960 to about 50,000 in 1990.[7] Côte d'Ivoire became, wags said, even more French after independence. French food was readily available and the language was widely spoken. If you went to Paris, one joke went, it would remind you of Abidjan. At the same time, Boigny's decision to focus on agriculture paid off.[8] Cocoa and coffee production rose. Money poured into the Treasury and Côte d'Ivoire thrived.

The government invested in public works and infrastructure. The port at Abidjan, the commercial capital, became one of Africa's busiest. A network of roads linked Ivorian ports to the landlocked hinterland of Niger, Mali and Burkina Faso. A railway connected Abidjan to Ouagadougou, the Burkinabe capital. Skyscrapers dotted the capital, which overlooked a lagoon where tourists water-skied. The immense Hotel Ivoire boasted West Africa's only ice rink. Per capita income rose from $70 at independence in 1960 to $610 in 1988.[9] International observers began to call Côte d'Ivoire a miracle. The country was seen as a place of calm and prosperity in a troubled region. By 1979, it had become the world's biggest cocoa producer.

The Ivorian elite and French investors profited hugely from the boom. Boigny lived in a $12 million palace, with fifty-two types of marble and an air-conditioned wine cellar.[10] Signs of hubris abounded. In his home village of Yamassoukro, he built a replica of St Peter's Basilica in Rome. About 1,500 workers toiled for three years to construct it, guides tell visitors. On completion in 1989, tourists came in busloads to visit the air-conditioned Basilica in the Bush, its grey dome visible for miles around. They followed the quiet footsteps of the guide on the muffled gleam of polished wood and marble. Boigny insisted he had paid for the Basilica himself.[11] When asked how much it cost, guides quoted Boigny, who said: 'Quant Dieu a l'homme, Dieu ne compte pas.' No price can be put on a gift from God.

But by the time the Basilica was completed, Boigny's miracle had begun to crack. When cocoa prices were high, he had spent heavily. When they fell, he borrowed. By the late 1980s, the country's debts totalled more than $8bn.[12] Short of cash, Côte d'Ivoire suspended payments on its debt in 1987.[13] In 1989, Boigny took the advice of the International Monetary Fund and World Bank and cut by half the payments to coffee and cocoa farmers to balance the country's books.[14]

For decades, French leaders had seen the Ivorian president as a reliable friend in West Africa. Politicians including Jean-Marie le Pen, the racist leader, and Socialist Party bigwigs had turned to him for advice. Jacques Foccart, President de Gaulle's adviser on African affairs, had a lifelong friendship with the president, speaking with him every Wednesday. 'He never caused blood to flow, and he let fewer of his opponents rot in prison than others did', Foccart later wrote in praise of Boigny.[15]

With his long stint in French government, Boigny was seen as part of the old-boy network of French politicians. They focused on his friendship, the country's stability and steady growth. But Côte d'Ivoire was a one-party state that never held elections, and as the economy crumbled opposition to Boigny fermented.

The cocoa boom had been made possible by Boigny's liberal interpretation of land laws and his open arms to immigrants.

Migrants bought or leased land from Western ethnic groups such as the Bete or Guere, many of whom worked in Abidjan. When the economy deteriorated, they returned home in search of land. 'Suddenly cocoa prices drop through the floor and the economy is not growing. Everyone wants to go back to the land', one exporter in Abidjan said. 'The problem is who owns it.' These tensions were keenly felt in the cocoa heartlands. In most cases this land had been sold, but locals spoke as if it had been taken. 'People realised land was given away', one official in Daloa said. 'They didn't have control of that land anymore; they realised it was needed for new generations and the people who were on it didn't want to give it away.'

Laurent Gbagbo, one of the first politicians openly to challenge Boigny, capitalised on this discontent.[16] In 1990, he stood against Boigny in the country's first multiparty elections, the only candidate to do so. His campaign accused the government of favouring foreigners.[17] Boigny won convincingly, but it was to be his last victory.

Three years after the elections, the 88-year-old president died of cancer. French politicians lined up to pay their respects. In attendance at his funeral at the Basilica in Yamoussoukro were French president François Mitterrand, prime minister Edouard Balladur, former president Valéry Giscard d'Estaing and six former prime ministers.[18] Outside, thousands of people had gathered to pay homage to a man they called *Le Sage*, *le Vieux* or *Nana*, a term in Baoule for 'grandfather'. Boigny had been lionised in a song by Alpha Blondy, a local reggae star, for looking after *nous ses petits*.

To this day, many Ivorians talk of what Boigny did for them and their country. Boigny himself had attributed his popularity to the fact he could interact easily with peasant farmers, French politicians and global businessmen. 'Traditional chieftains trusted me because I was one of them', he once said. 'So did the educated, modern-minded elite, because I was one of them, too.'[19] Boigny had dextrously manipulated links between France and West Africa. He had balanced the demand of the sixty or so different ethnic groups in Côte d'Ivoire and masterminded the creation of a state so economically successful and politically stable that for most of his rule it was referred to as a miracle. At the time of his death, he was Africa's longest-serving leader and the third-longest-serving in the world after Cuba's Fidel Castro and North Korea's Kim Il-Sung. Many wondered simply what would come next.

After Boigny – a crisis of identity

It is October 2007 and it is fourteen years after Boigny's death. The grey and purple seats of the eight o'clock bus from Daloa in western Côte d'Ivoire to Abidjan are full. Businessmen in shirts and ties, men in colourful traditional dress and mothers with small children are crushed inside. One man places his legs on top of the box in front of him. Another, his eyes shut, says prayers in Arabic. A woman puts her long legs and artfully painted toenails in the aisle. A baby in purple pants and gold hoop earrings gurgles. The seats are small. The aisle is narrow. Eggshells, plastic wrappers and soiled white tissues are scattered on the floor. Only a few windows work. As the bus picks up speed, air freshens our faces. Barely twenty minutes later, the bus slows as a road block comes into sight. The temperature rises. The bus falls silent as a soldier enters.

A gun slung on his back and beads of sweat on his face, he examines the papers of the headscarfed girl in seat 33. 'This says the year 2004', he said. 'We are in 2007.' Outside the bus, her brother pays 200 CFA to compensate for her out-of-date ID. I hold up my Irish passport for inspection. Those next to me hold up slips of paper, which on closer inspection are revealed to be either out of date or irrelevant. At each barrier, the same people face the same questions. Nobody fights their case. Polite and nervous, they count out the coins that allow them to proceed to the next stage of the journey.

In my naivety, I had chosen to travel on a bigger bus. I assumed it would move faster and make fewer stops. But I had underestimated the number of roadblocks. Private vehicles are often just waved through these barriers in a matter of minutes. They can do the journey from Daloa to Abidjan in four hours. On public transport, the journey takes twice as long. There are simply far more papers to check. For the brother and sister in front of me, the cost is not just wasted time. The 200 CFA they pay every time they get out of the bus quickly adds up. After six stops, I give up counting.

Ivorian politics can be bewilderingly complex. There appears to be a multitude of different interests and a permanently shifting set of alliances. I frequently struggled to follow the exact sequence of events. After Boigny's death, ethnic identity assumed a huge and divisive importance. During his rule, many in the north and west resented the fact that power remained in the hands of a southern Catholic elite. While Boigny had welcomed migrants, their legal status remained unclear. After his death these issues bubbled to the surface. What part of Côte d'Ivoire you came from and what papers you had became defining factors in Ivorian politics. Politicians vying for power started to talk about *Ivoirité*, what makes a true Ivorian. About one-quarter of the country's population are believed to be non-citizens, many of whom were born in Burkina Faso. Many are Dioula and frequently viewed by southerners as not truly Ivorian.[20] In a country with such a high proportion of immigrants, the concept of *Ivoirité* was to become a matter of life and death.

After Boigny's death, Côte d'Ivoire quickly entered a downward spiral. A handful of contenders vyed to succeed him. Henri Konan Bedié, the head of the national assembly, was his constitutional successor. Alassane Ouattara, the prime minister and a Muslim who came from the north, was his immediate rival. When Bedié became president, Ouattara resigned and the ruling party, a mixture of southern Christians and northern Muslims, split.

The new president began to ask questions about Ouattara's origins.[21] Was Ouattara, a reformer popular in the West who had worked for the IMF in Washington, a closet foreigner? Was a Muslim from the north with an allegedly Burkinabe parent truly Ivorian? The question was politically motivated. Ouattara was his main rival for the top job. But in a country once proud to open its borders to people across the region, this question of identity goes right to the heart of politics. At times, it can feel that nearly everyone in Côte d'Ivoire is from somewhere else. In securing his grip on power, Bedié had let the ethnic genie out of the bottle.

These accusations influenced relationships in plantations, villages and towns. Northerners whose names were often similar to Burkinabe or Malian names came under suspicion. Many immigrants, even those whose families had lived there for generations, did not have birth certificates, identity cards and passports. Soldiers arrested them at roadblocks. Many were only freed once they had handed over some cash.

Matters came to a head on Christmas Eve 1999. Gunshots rang out across the Plateau, the upmarket business district of Abidjan. Rebels took control of the airport, the port and radio and television headquarters as troops and hooligans pillaged the capital.[22] Until then, Côte d'Ivoire and Senegal had been the only two countries in West Africa not to have had a coup. As General Robert Guei, called *Le Boss* by soldiers, took power, President Bedié fled to Togo. There was a deep sense of shock in Abidjan. This was the first time this had happened in nearly forty years of independent rule. 'This was unprecedented', one journalist in the capital at the time said. People were stunned by the car-jackings, the armed robberies and the looting. No one understood quite how significant these events would prove to be. 'I think people didn't realise that Côte d'Ivoire would never be the same again. There was just no experience of political instability. They couldn't quite comprehend the fact that it was all over', he added.

Elections were held the following year but were dominated by the debate over ethnic identity. Both Guei and Gbagbo stood but a court ruled that Ouattara was not Ivorian and thus ineligible to stand. When voting booths did open, just over a third of voters turned out to vote. Voting was particularly low in the north, the natural constituency of Ouattara, the banned candidate. Nearly two-thirds of those who did make it to the ballot box supported Gbagbo.[23] General Guei tried to declare himself the winner, but Gbagbo's supporters took to the streets in protest, and within days their candidate had installed himself as president. Faced with calls for an election which included Ouattara on the ballot, Mr Gbagbo's followers attacked Muslim areas in Abidjan. In one incident on the edge of the city, more than fifty men were killed, their bodies dumped in a forest.[24]

Happy to see Guei gone, many people simply did not recognise Gbagbo's victory. 'One-third of the Ivorian population cannot choose a president', said Sekou Kone, an Abidjan merchant who hid in his shop from the violence that had erupted on the streets.[25] Observers agreed. The UN, the USA and the Organization of African Unity called for new elections.[26] But France, still the main powerbroker in the country, declared itself satisfied with the result. Gbagbo had close links with the French Socialist Party. Michel Rocard, a former prime minister under President Mitterand, welcomed 'our comrade' Gbagbo to the presidency.[27]

Tensions continued to simmer. Nearly two years later, in the early hours of 19 September 2002, northern rebels led by Guillaume Soro, an obscure student leader, tried to take power. Soro made clear their anger stemmed from their lack of official recognition. 'Give us our identity cards and we hand over our Kalashnikovs', he said. The insurgents killed the home affairs minister responsible for new identity cards that led to many people losing their right to vote.[28] The rebels failed to take over the capital but took control of the northern half of Côte d'Ivoire. The country split in two.

The attempted coup reverberated far beyond Ivorian borders. Relationships with neighbouring countries and France began to fracture. Both France and Burkina Faso were suspected of backing the rebels. France sent troops to keep the peace, stressing that it supported Gbagbo's government. Gbagbo condemned France's involvement as a neocolonial plot. The house built by Boigny had come crashing down. The impact of the rebellion was keenly felt in the south-west, where tensions over land had been building for decades.

Battle for land

When news of war broke, Thomas was on a bus bound for Duékoué. At a roadblock outside the town of Boauflé, a local militia ordered northerners off the vehicle, targeting those with names similar to rebel leaders. 'Your leader Ouattara is the one who is going to take the power from us', one fighter told Thomas. Thomas pressed coins and notes into their hands and was allowed to continue his journey. Overnight, dozens of roadblocks had been thrown up. Some were organised by soldiers, others by bands of local youths. A trip that normally took one day took three. By the time Thomas reached his home town, the slow-burning tensions on land ownership had been set ablaze by the northern attack. 'There was only one question in Duékoué', said Thomas. 'How to claim our land back from the foreigners.'

This was fertile land, planted with cocoa and coffee and farmed by people from all over Côte d'Ivoire and West Africa. Complex relationships over land and labour had fuelled this boom. In Ghana and Côte d'Ivoire, producers paid for access to land with labour, a share of the crops or cash. While in Ghana rows over land are rarely politically charged, in Côte d'Ivoire Boigny himself had been forced to intervene in disputes between local people and migrants. In the 1970s, the government brutally suppressed an uprising in the south-west, as locals complained that the state favoured migrants.[29]

Attempts to resolve disputes over land ownership in Côte d'Ivoire have been fraught. In the late 1990s, President Bedié's administration, backed by the World Bank, started to map and register rural land rights. A draft 1998 law went a step further. Under the Loi Foncier, those with traditional or customary rights to land would be able to register them. There was considerable confusion about what this meant for immigrants. Egged on by politicians, violent clashes erupted in the south-west. In September 1999, more than 10,000 people were expelled from their land and villages. No one in authority did anything to protect them.[30]

By the time war broke out in 2002, emotions about foreigners were running high. Politicians and newspapers accused the Burkinabe of backing the rebels. Local farmers chased immigrants from their plantations, destroying receipts for land purchase and documents confirming official land usage.[31] Across the cocoa-growing south-west, both sides waged tit-for-tat attacks.[32]

Behind closed doors in Duékoué, I was shown pictures of farmers brutalised by militias and of smallholders killed by immigrants. Their skin had been burnt, their hands were tied behind their backs and their dead eyes were open in shock. In the government press, these attacks were portrayed as spontaneous attempts to reclaim land from rebel sympathisers. But many blamed politicians' inflammatory comments for inciting the violence. By early April 2003, militias were effectively in control of Duékoué.[33] 'They were picking people up and killing them', one northerner, resident in the town, told me. 'There were people in uniform who picked them; they used to pick people who were northerners.' He added: 'They just aimed at the Dioula people, the Muslims and the northerners.' Even if the government did not actively support these militias, many believed that, at the very least, it tolerated them.[34]

Nothing stopped the flow of cocoa from plantations around the country. In spite of the rebellion, the roadblocks and the murder of farmers, beans continued to move to the port. 'It surprised all of us – the first concern was that the cocoa would go down [because of the rebellion] but it didn't happen, one exporter said. As smallholders fled, those who took their places sold the fruit of their harvest. These beans were needed to keep production lines in Amsterdam, Germany and America functioning. This produce was often of poor quality, but one buyer in Guiglo, near the town of Duékoué, said: 'We had no choice [but to take it] we needed the product.'

No one wanted the movement of cocoa to stop. 'Cocoa has been almost like a lifeline to this country. Everybody can make their margin, the government can get its revenue, the police get their revenue, so does the *traitant*', one exporter told me. It was in no one's interest for the beans to stay on the farm. The hundreds of thousands of producers who needed the crop to survive would have been hurt if international buyers had stopped purchases, he argued. 'It wouldn't have helped to stop buying cocoa; you would have hurt innocent peasants; it wouldn't have solved the problem.' One human rights activist in Daloa told me: 'Cocoa is the spoils of war, it has accentuated it, it did not light it, it is an old system.' The real issues are land and identity, he said. Thomas's father became fatally intertwined in this struggle.

In the graveyard

The day Thomas's father went missing, a funeral was taking place in Duékoué. A man killed by immigrant farmers was being buried. Many feared there could be a reprisal attack. Police barriers had been moved, a sign interpreted by Thomas that danger was imminent. As the day progressed and there was no sign of his father, Thomas became increasingly anxious. When darkness fell, he decided to look for him. Not far from the centre of town, he spotted something on the road. He braked. On the ground in front of him was the sack his father used to carry coffee in, the sack he had left the house with. Nearby were his father's shoes.

Thomas went home and resumed the search for his father the next day. This time, he went to the graveyard. Near the grave of the fighter buried the day before, Thomas saw the stone his father used to sharpen his machete, the rubber he used to tie his goods to his bicycle, scattered metal cases from bullets and splashes of blood. He began to dig. Beneath the coffin of the dead fighter, he could see an arm. He jumped into the grave and started to pull a body out. The toes had been cut off, the fingers hacked, the ears severed and the scalp sliced. There were machete wounds so deep that they revealed the bone of the leg. The badly mutilated body was pocked by bullets. Thomas recognised the corpse as that of his father.

I met Thomas eleven months after his father's death. An official in a nearby town told me about the case and I asked for his contact number. His story stood out for me but it was, the official assured me, by no means an unusual one. When I first saw Thomas, he was sitting quietly listening to a Walkman while I spoke with a relative. He joined our conversation on the faded pink veranda of his cousin's house. When he started to speak, I was struck by how intense, quietly spoken and articulate he was.

I had been told that someone had been jailed for the murder. But Thomas doubted that the man in jail was really the killer. The authorities support the militias, he said. They were unlikely to punish the culprit. He wanted to talk but struggled with the memory of what had happened. 'If he had died normally, we would have said it was an act of God', said Thomas. 'But he was brutally murdered; when we see how he was cut, it is very difficult to forget it.' He misses his father, who woke him up in the morning to pray. He also had other pressures. Money was tight. His mother followed her husband to the grave within months. Thomas has seventeen relatives to provide for. Thomas felt his father's killer was someone who knew him and who knew his family. He felt he was being watched. We waited until the road outside was clear before we left his cousin's compound. Local journalists cannot be trusted, he added. They were government spies. He hoped that speaking to an international reporter would help him secure justice for his father, but he did not want me to use his real name in case the authorities found out he had spoken to me.

I understood his caution. If you are the only white person in a small African town it is common for people to be curious. This interest is usually overwhelmingly friendly. But what I experienced in Duékoué was different. Wherever I went, I felt I was being observed. In my hotel restaurant I ended a phone call when I noted the waitress listening intently. I had Nescafé coffee for breakfast in a maquis, a local restaurant, but put my notebook away when I realised other customers were watching me write. On my second night in town, politicians arrived for a rally. My driver suggested we move to a hotel on the outskirts of Duékoué so as not to attract attention to ourselves. No one I met wanted to speak at their offices or home. They were afraid someone they knew would spot them with a white journalist. During one interview in a hotel function room, a government official stopped talking when he heard a cleaner in the next room. He feared a spy had followed him and was listening to our conversation. People made time to speak with me but few, immigrant or local, felt able to speak openly. Many people had warned me about Duékoué before I went there. They all said the same thing: the situation was tense because of the battle for land.

It was in Duékoué also that the arguments about identity and origins seemed to be the most intensely felt and confused. The person who suggested I meet Thomas described him as Burkinabe. Yet Thomas insists that he is an Ivorian national and that he has all the documents he needs to prove that he is Ivorian. My driver dismisses Thomas's claim to be Ivorian and said that most of 'these people' are confused about their origins. Even if Thomas is from within Côte d'Ivoire, many in Duékoué would in any case refer to him as an *allogene*. He is a person from another part of Côte d'Ivoire. He is not Bete or Guere. He did not originate from the west. He is a foreigner.

Whichever part of Côte d'Ivoire you come from, people are quick to assign traits to you. The Baoule, Boigny's people, 'were the most motivated, the most interested in the land', one northerner told me. He added that 'when he [Boigny] said those

who cultivate it can keep it, it was the Baoule he meant.' Some
of these perceptions clearly have their root in colonial times. The
French encouraged the Baoule to adopt export crops because of
their 'wealth-producing aptitude'. The Baoule see themselves as
hard-working and sophisticated and perceive the people from
the west as uneducated people who waste money. The Guere
'don't work hard, they can be a bit violent', one said. Another
added: 'Guere people mainly work to eat, they don't have great
commercial will.' For the Guere, the 'foreign' farmers were at
best usurpers, at worst accomplices of the rebels. They are
helping the insurgents, one Guere woman told me. 'That is why
they do not let the original owners go to their farms', she said.
Politicians have manipulated these stereotypes. 'The crisis is not
the problem of the population, it is the problem of politicians',
one human rights activist, also quick to condemn the Guere as
lazy, told me. 'The population have been poor for a long time,
but it is the politicians who manipulated it. Every time there is
a problem, the people are turned against the foreigners.' This
view was common right across Côte d'Ivoire. A rebel in Bouake
told me: 'We could all be Ivorian if the government wanted us
[to be].'

Land and identity

In Côte d'Ivoire, the papers you have can determine your right to
own land, to move freely and to vote. With the right papers, you
can call Côte d'Ivoire your home. With the wrong ones, you are
effectively stateless, no matter how long you or your family have
lived there. The issue of who is or isn't Ivorian lies at the heart
of the country's insecurity and has led not just to thousands of
deaths but also to the displacement of hundreds of thousands of
people.

The war itself lasted barely a year, ending in 2003. But the country remained split in two by an artificial border manned by UN and French troops until 2007. In March that year, President Gbagbo signed a peace deal with Guillaume Soro, the rebel leader. Mr Soro became prime minister and the former adversaries agreed to disarm, reunify and hold an election. But these polls have been repeatedly postponed, due to problems with voter registration, an issue closely linked with the issue of identity. Northern rebel commanders still control their own fiefdoms. Thousands of pro-government militias have not disarmed.[35] Many still do not have papers or secure tenure. Most of the thousands of displaced farmers have returned to their plantations, but the vast majority of immigrant landholders do not have officially recognised rights to the land they farm.

The underlying issues in the conflict remain difficult to resolve. Those indigenous to the area want their land back or at least a source of income away from the land. Many feel they gave away too much and received too little in return. Thomas wants a law that secures him access to the land his father bought and that his family has farmed for more than thirty years. For a politician eager to sow discord, this south-western corner of Côte d'Ivoire is fertile ground. Identity and land tenure will matter in Ivorian politics and life long after any election is held.

In the months after Thomas's father's death, a neighbouring farmer told him that he, not Thomas, is the rightful owner of his land. Thomas is an outsider and should not be able to inherit land, he says. His neighbour knew the original owner of the plantation. As Thomas's father is dead, the neighbour says, the land now belongs to him. Thomas wondered if this man had been involved in his father's death. But Thomas is not prepared to give up the land for which his father died. He knows who he is and where he is from. 'I am an Ivorian, I am an Ivorian wherever I choose to establish myself, I have built my own house, I cannot give it up … I have everything an Ivorian can have: a birth cert, a nationality cert, an identity card. I have both my mother's and my father's birth certificate', he said. 'Nobody can take me from here, not with a bulldozer, not with a tractor.'

THREE

CHILD LABOUR

The crusading senator

When Tom Harkin, the Democratic senator for the state of Iowa, visited an Ivorian cocoa village in early 2008, he was shocked by how little farmers had. The people he met lacked clean water, health care and decent schools for their children. 'They are so far out in the middle of nowhere, their first priority was getting drinking water', he said. These producers wanted to build a future for their families, he said, but they couldn't see a way forward. 'They had a makeshift school, it was really bad, they had nothing ... No books, or very few books. It was pretty stark, they are saying we want our kids to go to school. But we don't have them, we need teachers.'[1]

Born in 1939, the grey-haired politician has spent much of his political life doing what he can to get children out of work and into school. Over the past several decades, he has championed Bangladeshi children who stitch garments and Pakistani children who make footballs. As a child, the senator, the son of a coal-miner, delivered papers and worked on farms and construction sites. He speaks with passion about helping children get the best chance in life. They need to 'learn to read and write and know basic math', he said. That way, he said, they have 'saleable skills'. Since 2001, he has devoted his efforts to improving the lot of under-age labourers on cocoa farms in West Africa.

Child labour on cocoa plantations first came to public attention with a string of newspaper reports about slavery in 2000. Traffickers preyed on children at bus stops in Mali, promising riches on cocoa farms in Côte d'Ivoire.[2] Once children got to the farm, they survived on little food, little or no pay and endured regular beatings.[3] There were no chains and no irons, but, unable to leave their place of work, they were effectively slaves, harvesting the beans that were the key ingredient for chocolate.

For the senator, the contrast between the lives of these producers and the deep pockets of chocolate companies such as Mars and Hershey is a clear injustice. Chocolate companies needed to act. 'The amounts of money we are talking about [to eradicate child labour] are not large in comparison to [the] worldwide profits they make', he said, the frustration evident in his voice. 'If the price of a Hershey bar went up two cents, or Mars two cents, and that money was just devoted to eradication of child labour, they would have more than enough.' Fearing the impact of bad publicity on sales, the chocolate industry promised to survey conditions on plantations and end child labour. In 2001, they signed the Harkin–Engel protocol, a voluntary agreement named after the senator and Congressman Eliot Engel.

But nearly a decade later, very little has actually changed on the farm. Progress has been slow, the senator admits. Untangling why sheds light on the reality of life in a cocoa-farming village. It also illuminates the inner workings of the industry. If fewer children are to work on smallholdings, then cocoa farming itself needs to change. Reducing the number of children on plantations requires a wholesale reform of the cocoa business.

Industry cynicism

Shortly before I left London to move to Ghana in 2005, a colleague at Reuters introduced me to an industry contact. We went for lunch to talk about cocoa, but mostly what we talked about was child labour.

The executive, who had long experience of West Africa, was furious with the senator's campaign, which was then four years old. He believed it to be wrong-headed and foolish. Children may work on cocoa farms, he said, but they certainly weren't slaves. There were just as many children working as household help or in the fishing industry. Large chocolate companies were an easy target for journalists or activists too lazy to try to really understand the industry, he told me.

That lunch meeting was the first of many where I heard such views. Many voiced anger at overhyped media reports, which they said exaggerated the existence of slavery and child labour. One executive told me: 'I think people are completely mad; I used to work on a farm in the holidays. It is absolutely ridiculous ... I find it just a joke. It is completely overhyped.... It is a great pity, it [this campaign] has done no one any favours.'

Ghanaian and Ivorian officials voiced much the same opinion. Most children on African farms are working with their parents, Madame Amoun Acquah, the Ivorian government spokeswoman on child labour and cocoa, told me haughtily in a busy Abidjan hotel, above the buzz of mid-morning chatter. There are few trafficked children on farms, she said. Children are engaged in an apprenticeship on their parents' plantations, she said. Here in Africa, she added, weary of explaining these basic facts to visiting journalists, our school is the plantation.

In an African household, everyone contributes to the family's welfare, a Ghanaian buyer told me. He had accompanied his mother to the farm from the age of 5. 'We didn't do anything serious but just keep her company and carry some food and she would work', he said. 'The reality on the ground was we had to help our fathers do all those things and still get some education.' Helping out is an important part of growing up, he added.

> Even if you are going to school, go and help in the farm. That would be your contribution to the farm, which would essentially pay for all the facilities you enjoy at school. They have to know how the parents are suffering to see them through school, to also see how hard work is rewarded at the end of the day.

Children also work in France and America, added Côte d'Ivoire's Madame Acquah. This was overheated and sentimental, she indicated. 'It is emotional, it is chocolate, it is children', she said.

Some of these responses made sense. Clearly, there was nothing wrong with helping out your family on the farm, or learning how to grow cocoa. But others struck me as fairly graceless. None of the executives, European or African, I spoke to, had sacrificed their education or prospects to support their family. Whatever work they had done as children, they had still received an education that had equipped them for life. In contrast, those I met who hadn't been to school spoke movingly about what the loss of an education meant to them. One man, who was kept out of school to work for his father, told me: 'Being an illiterate has cost me in so many ways.... There may be opportunities for literate people; I cannot have them because I am illiterate, people wouldn't give me a chance; I feel I am missing a lot.'

Chocolate companies had a lot to lose from the media's interest in child labour. Their businesses rested on the sale and shipment of beans from the Gulf of Guinea. They also feared the impact of these stories on consumer sales. 'They live in fear of the headline which could lead to the boycott', one industry lobbyist told me.

Economic fear also fuelled the Ghanaian and Ivorian response to these reports. Hundreds of thousands of people rely on this crop. It is one of their biggest export earners. Alhassan Osman, a fellow at Accra's University of Ghana, who researched child labour for Swedwatch, an NGO, said officials kept silent over Ghana's child labour problem for fear it would hurt the sector. 'For a country like Ghana, where the economy still thrives on cocoa, some officials say that saying [child labour] exists might lead to an embargo, it might cast a slur on the cocoa we export', he said. The senator's campaign had clearly rattled a lot of people. Many believed he had simply exaggerated the extent of the problem.

Defining the problem

From the beginning, it has been hard to establish how many children work on cocoa farms and what exactly they do. The senator made clear he had no problem with family labour as such. 'On Saturdays that is OK. I might even go a step further, sometimes during a harvest season, if a kid has to take a couple of days off school, I am not going to shout and scream about that', he reasoned. His concerns centred on slavery and children who worked in dangerous conditions.

Those who signed up to the Harkin–Engel protocol promised to identify and eliminate the worst forms of child labour as defined by International Labour Organization (ILO) Convention 182. This definition includes slavery and hazardous work. Hazardous work, according to ILO Convention 182, is 'work which, by its nature or the circumstances in which it is carried out, is likely to harm the health, safety or morals of children.' On the cocoa plantation, this is generally defined to include work which involves dangerous machinery, equipment or tools, the handling of heavy loads and exposure to pesticides or chemicals. According to ILO definitions, child labour refers to those under 15 who are economically active and those between 15 and 17 who are involved in dangerous work. Light work for children aged between 12 and 14 is considered acceptable so long as it doesn't exceed fourteen hours a week.

Those who went in search of trafficked children on cocoa farms could certainly find them, but initial estimates of the extent of slavery on cocoa farms varied widely. One interviewee in a British documentary suggested that as many as 90 per cent of Ivorian farms used slave labour.[4] This implied there were hundreds of thousands of slaves in Côte d'Ivoire. A BBC report suggested that 15,000 children were in slavery on these plantations.[5]

But surveys found that producers overwhelmingly used family labour. 'The recruitment and employment of both children and adults from outside the family as permanent salaried workers was relatively uncommon', according to a comprehensive survey of the sector, carried out in 2002 by the International Institute of Tropical Agriculture (IITA).[6] About 12,000 children on planta-tions in Côte d'Ivoire were estimated to have no family ties nearby, a warning sign they could have been trafficked. Roughly 2,100 working children were recruited through intermediaries for cocoa farming in Côte d'Ivoire. Relative to the huge numbers of people who worked in cocoa, the incidence of slavery appeared to be slight. But hundreds of thousands of children did work on cocoa farms, often doing risky work. The IITA estimated that there were nearly 300,000 children working in hazardous conditions, carrying loads that were too heavy for them or ap-plying pesticides.

A later study, carried out by Tulane University[7] and published in 2009 – the third in a series of reports by the University – estimated that more than 800,000 children in Côte d'Ivoire and nearly 1 million children in Ghana had worked on cocoa-related activities in the previous twelve months. Across both countries, there were more than 500,000 working in breach of ILO guidelines and national laws on minimum age and minimum hours, 263,000 in Côte d'Ivoire and 270,000 in Ghana. Working children mostly weeded, harvested cocoa and carried beans to the shed, it found. More than half reported an injury. 'Children working in the cocoa sector sometimes are exposed to activities classified as hazardous by the governments of Côte d'Ivoire and Ghana, including frequent involvement in land clearing, carrying of heavy loads', the report noted. Again, there appeared to be little evidence of slavery. Cases of debts or the need to work to pay off debts are very rare, it said. About 5 per cent of children in Côte d'Ivoire and 10 per cent in Ghana worked for pay. Some people were forced to work, but usually by a relative. Less than 0.5 per cent of children in agricultural households had been forced to work by a non-relative, it found.

At the same time, a lot of these children were in school. Roughly 60 per cent of children in Côte d'Ivoire and 90 per cent in Ghana were in the educational system, including, the report said, a large number of working children. Just because these children had enrolled didn't mean they were regular attendees. In both countries, it found that about 40 per cent of children between 5 and 17 years could not read or write a short simple statement.

It also appeared that children in cocoa-growing areas were *more* likely to attend school than others. In Côte d'Ivoire, 45 per cent of those aged between 5 and 17 outside of cocoa-growing areas had attended school. This figure jumps to 58 per cent in the cocoa belt. In Ghana, 74 per cent of children in this age group outside of cocoa-growing areas had attended school. This contrasted with 89 per cent in agricultural households in the crop's heartlands.

Children clearly worked elsewhere as well. In Accra, I saw children working as cleaners, vendors and shoe-shiners. The fare collectors on local transport, known as tro-tros, were frequently young boys, hanging out of the side of their battered vehicles, shouting for customers. Others worked as porters and domestic servants. At the beach at the weekend, I saw small boys helping fishermen haul in nets. Officials at the International Organization for Migration told me there was a problem with child slavery in Ghana, but on fishing villages in the country's east, not on cocoa plantations.

The picture painted by the Tulane survey was a complex one. Children did work on cocoa farms, but many also went to school. They sometimes worked in hazardous conditions and frequently worked long hours. But these were poor countries and it wasn't clear to me that these children were automatically worse off than others in Ghana and Côte d'Ivoire. UNICEF, the United Nations childrens' agency, estimates that 35 per cent of children aged between 5 and 14 in Côte d'Ivoire[8] and 34 per cent of children aged between 5 and 14 in Ghana[9] do some work.

I began to understand the scathing comments voiced by people in the industry about campaigners. Many reports were muddled and exaggerated. In early February 2010, the American Federation of Teachers (AFT) noted that 'for 3.6 million children in Ghana and Côte d'Ivoire, Valentine's Day will be just another desolate day of harvesting cocoa under inexcusable conditions.' The AFT called for an end to the import of 'child-harvested cocoa beans'.[10] Professor Lennard Davis of the University of Illinois, Chicago, wrote on the influential *Huffington Post* website that 'more than half of the world's chocolate comes from these areas in Africa in which children under 14 do brutally heavy work, apply pesticides, are hurt by machetes, unfair labour practices, and many of them are actually slaves stolen from their families.' He put the number of children on African farms at 6.3 million and advised concerned consumers to buy Fairtrade or chocolate that has come from anywhere other than Africa.[11] An Oxfam campaign in Belgium advised consumers to buy Fairtrade chocolate, which accounts for 1 per cent of chocolate sold there, as other manufacturers could not guarantee beans had not been harvested by children. This was widely interpreted by local media as meaning that the cocoa in 99 per cent of chocolate sold in Belgium could have been picked by children, many of them slaves.

In practice, the use of the terms 'slavery' or 'trafficking' to describe the migration of children in search of work obscures a complex cultural reality. An article published in the *British Medical Journal* shows that often so-called traffickers are intermediaries who help children make the journey safely.[12] While many are exploited, others are not. Some undertake the trip not out of financial necessity but because it is a rite of passage. Sometimes children who have been returned to their home villages by well-meaning charities leave again in search of work, research carried out for the London School of Hygiene & Tropical Medicine found. Researchers feared that tougher rules on trafficking would not deter children but force them to take illicit or dangerous routes. In this context, it is not difficult to understand Ghanaian and Ivorian anger. Exaggerated or simplified media reports paint a picture few people recognise and serve little purpose other than to raise hackles.

It is also doubtful a boycott of 'slave-produced' beans would make matters better. A ban on beans from the region would devastate millions of families reliant on cocoa to survive. These kinds of threats or bans, however well-intentioned, can backfire dramatically. The Harkin Bill was introduced into Congress in 1992 with the aim of prohibiting the import of products made by children under the age of 15. The mere threat of such a bill panicked the garment industry in Bangladesh, which exported 60 per cent of their products to the USA. Child workers, mostly girls, were sacked from the garment factories. Many ended up in worse conditions. 'Some were found working in more hazardous situations, in unsafe workshops where they were paid less, or in prostitution', according to UNICEF's *The State of the World's Children* report for 1997. It was, the report noted, a classic case of good motives gone wrong.

In practice, it is hard to implement a slavery-free label for cocoa, even though similar schemes have worked well with other products. With the Rugmark label, now known as GoodWeave, looms are regularly checked and there is a credible inspection system in place to ensure that no children are involved in making these rugs.

It is, however, genuinely difficult to check if children are working on hundreds of thousands of scattered plantations. In West Africa, farms are owned by individual farmers, not large chocolate companies. These producers take their beans to the nearest buying station, often several miles away, and sell them to whichever middleman has available cash. In both countries, international companies such as Mars or Cadbury are not allowed to buy beans directly from producers upcountry. It is not unheard of for companies to breach these laws in Côte d'Ivoire, but remote smallholdings are rarely checked by officials in either country.

'You think about having 2 million small-scale farmers, scattered over remote areas of West Africa, you don't know what happens every day on a cocoa farm', said Bill Guyton, president of the

World Cocoa Foundation, 'I don't know if there is any model in the cocoa sector which can guarantee 100 per cent.' At the same time, few chocolate bars are made from beans from a single village or producer. Most are mixed in with others to create different flavours. Any one tablet contains beans from farms scattered all over the world. Once you start to unravel the trail of ingredients in a single bar, it is difficult to say with certainty that no children were exploited in its production.

Some buyers are trying to provide this kind of traceability and reassurance for cocoa. They include Kuapa Kokoo, the Fairtrade (see Chapter 6) buyer in Ghana; Armajaro; and Mars. These schemes often exist on a small scale and come with caveats. Cargill, the American cocoa processor, has worked with Utz Certified to train 1,500 farmers in responsible and sustainable production practices. Annual output of the Utz scheme totals 3,000 tonnes, a tiny fraction of Côte d'Ivoire's annual production of 1.2 million tonnes. Each individual farmer is checked every year but Utz makes clear that no 'scheme can give a completely watertight 100 per cent guarantee' that children did not harvest these beans.

Campaigners frequently direct shoppers to Fairtrade, yet officials at Kuapa Kokoo, the co-operative in Ghana, stop short of promising there are no children on these farms.[13] The difficulty of providing any kind of guarantee became clear in early 2010, when a British television report showed that in September 2009 the Fairtrade cocoa co-operative in Ghana had suspended seven out of thirty-three of their cocoa farming communities in one of its fifty-two districts found to be using the worst forms of child labour.[14] Fairtrade said the discovery was a sign that its regular checks was working. But it also made clear that such schemes are fraught with difficulties. Separately, the Tulane University report noted: 'The ability to verify a 100 per cent free [of the worst forms of child labour] environment is doubtful.'

Consumers increasingly want to know where their products come from and understandably don't want to buy goods made by children. But, said Jan Vingerhoets of the International Cocoa Organization (ICCO), this problem is too complex to be solved by a simple consumer initiative. 'I have not seen a farm family in the world that do not want their children to go to school. I have never met parents who do not want the best for their children', he said. Simply paying registered farmers more for beans won't make them better producers, he said. 'Make the farmers better farmers. Help them produce better food crops plus a cash crop. All parents want their children to have better chances. Child labour is an economic problem. Solve the poverty and you solve the child labour problem.' This is a problem that goes right to the heart of the cocoa industry and of rural poverty in Africa.

In search of riches

For someone who was only 12, Oussou Kwaku seems older than his years. He was keen to start earning money and eager to be an adult. When a stranger told his parents he could find their son work as a mechanic in Abidjan, he jumped at the chance. The youngest of twelve, his parents could not afford to educate him. This job could be a route to a better life. 'It was good to leave', he told me. 'I will grow up and really know the trade.'

But Kwaku's dream went quickly and badly wrong. He was forced to work on a palm-oil plantation from six in the morning until six at night. His arms ached from the work and, in return, he received just one meal a day. Six months later, he escaped to a neighbouring village, bitter and angry at the farmer who had exploited him.

Police and border authorities are increasingly on the lookout for children such as Kwaku. In Aboisso, an Ivorian town close to the Ghanaian border, police check for those who may be travelling unaccompanied or with false ID. Most of these children are not being taken against their will, one officer told me. Like Kwaku, many are not in school and want a new life, one where there is work, food and a future. Out of every ten children stopped on the border, he told me, at least eight are happy. They are happy to be leaving home and, like Kwaku, happy to be getting work.

In a large family, where food is scarce, it is easy to believe that life will be better for your children elsewhere. 'People have so many mouths to feed, any stranger who comes they want to offload that child, that extra mouth, because they think in this household, the child is worse off than if he goes with a stranger', Tony Dogbe, an NGO worker in Ghana, told me. 'They are not doing it with any malice; they think they are doing the child a favour. It is a bit like when people migrate from Ghana to Europe, they think you are going to the land of plenty.'

For children in Mali or Burkina Faso, which are much poorer than the southern state, the vision of riches in Côte d'Ivoire is enough to encourage them to leave their family. These two countries have a long history of migration to their wealthier neighbour. 'Children say going to Côte d'Ivoire to cocoa farms is like picking gold off the tree; they have a vision or fantasy of what they will get', another NGO worker added. Some children are lured by the promise of bicycles, clothes and money. 'They generally tend to be the third or last children of large families', she said. 'Children believe they can still get this money, this bicycle, these clothes. When they return, they are hugely disappointed, because they don't get any of it.'

Even when these plans go very badly wrong, the dream can remain very much alive. Asked what he wants to do now, Kwaku says he does not want to go home. He still wants to become a mechanic. He wants to work in a garage in Abidjan. The job he is chasing presents a better reality than the one he left behind.

I was introduced to Kwaku by an NGO which worked with trafficked children. It initially said he had worked on a cocoa farm. I do believe this was an innocent mistake on the part of people who were eager to help me. Kwaku quickly made clear he had worked in palm oil, not cocoa. But it made me wonder about NGO willingness to supply a victim to fit a convenient narrative. Several journalists wanted to meet children who had worked on cocoa farms. Far fewer were looking for those who worked on palm-oil plantations. In this light, industry fears that that they were being targeted because they sold a consumer good struck a chord.

Kwaku seemed tough and resilient. He had scarcely any education but was determined to make a better life for himself. He wanted a job, a chance to earn money and improve his life. It wasn't hard to see how he had fallen into the trap set for him by the unscrupulous trader. He couldn't see a future for himself in his home village. One of the best ways of keeping vulnerable children out of the hands of traffickers, one NGO worker told me, was to make sure they were in school. That way, they and their parents could see a future for them in their home village or town. And one of the best ways to ensure attendance in school was to provide food for children when they got there. That way, their parents face less pressure to take them out of education to earn money to survive.

School and the farm

For 16-year-old Alhassan Ali, work on a cocoa farm presented a chance to make a better life for himself. Encouraged by his mother, he left his home in Bolgatanga in northern Ghana in search of work when he was 14. 'I was told it rained a lot (in western Ghana) so there was always work. I thought I had relatives here', he says. Sitting quietly on a plastic chair in the village, his feet shuffling in yellow plastic sandals, he adds: 'I was hungry, I wasn't in school. I came on my own, nobody came for me.'

Shrouded in mist and forest on a rough red-dust road, Betenase seemed a surprising destination for job-seekers. It lacks running water and electricity. Its 1,500 inhabitants live mostly in mud dwellings. But Alhassan is not the only child from northern Ghana to have made the journey here. There are about twenty other children from the north living and working on smallholdings. A local woman regularly ferries children like Alhassan to the nearby town of Sefwi Wiawso, itself a low-rise muddle of shanty dwellings, where doughnuts bubble in fat over roadside stoves, yellow corn burns on open grills and fish heads press against dirty glass on streetside stalls. She refused to meet with me, but people in the town told me she brings children to work as shop assistants and househelp. Others work on cocoa farms.

In the week before we met, Alhassan had just finished breaking cocoa pods and putting beans to dry on woven trays. He had no idea what these beans are used for and has never tasted chocolate. All he knows is that the government buys them. When he has finished work on the plantation in the mid- to late afternoon, he heads back to the village. There he fetches water and pounds yams for fufu. For his labour, Alhassan earns an annual fee of 30 new Ghana cedis ($21).[15] Twice a day, he ate his fill, usually of fufu, banku, a ground corn dish, and ampesi, boiled yam and stew. At night, he shared a foam mattress with two other labourers in a mud hut with a zinc roof. A devout Muslim, he had Fridays off to pray. His employer treated him well, he told me.

But Alhassan clearly felt cheated. Life was hard in Betenase, he said, almost as hard as it is in northern Ghana. If his father had lived, he believes that he would have stayed in school and fulfilled his dream of becoming a commercial driver or a teacher. At least, he says, in Betenase he has a place to live and food to eat.

There is a school in the village but Alhassan is too busy working to attend. Ten-year-old Baba Arabas, his legs swinging shyly as he whispers his answers to questions, had just started going to school when I met him. Still baby-faced, it was hard to believe Baba had ever worked on a plantation. He simply seemed too young to be of real help on the farm. Visiting charity workers have paid for his uniform and books, after persuading Lamisi Kusasi, his uncle, to allow Baba to attend school. 'Baba is my brother's son', said Lamisi Kusasi, his uncle, who worked in Betenase for six years and is also from northern Ghana. 'The brother has so many children to look after, Baba has become a problem. He wanted me to bring Baba to help on the farm', he said, embarrassed to have to answer these questions. His intention had been to help Baba, he said. 'I did plan to send Baba to school. If he continued working, I would have given him part of the farm.'

Many in the village want their children to go to school, says Nana Kwaku Donkor, the village chief. This has been made easier by the abolition of primary school fees in 2005. But people still struggle to buy mandatory books and uniforms. Facilities are also poor. The school in Betenase has three classrooms for its one hundred children. Many smaller children take their lessons outdoors, where they sit on stools beneath a large tree.

Proud as Baba is of his school uniform, he says he has learnt hardly anything since he started school. We joke with him that he hasn't been paying attention until it becomes clear that the problem is that the teacher is rarely there. Baba still works weekends on the farm. He has to, laughs Nana Kwaku Donkor. 'If he doesn't come on Saturday, he will only have water during the week.'

I visited Betenase three times during 2007. On the third occasion, the reception was much cooler. Alhassan, Baba and Kusasi were gone and nobody would say to where. I had quoted them and mentioned Betenase in a report I had written for Reuters. The local NGO worker who travelled with me to the settlement to translate had warned me that the villagers were angry with me. After the report's publication, government officials had berated the villagers for making Ghana look bad and endangering its cocoa exports.

I often wondered what happened to Alhassan, Baba and Kusasi. Nobody I spoke to thought for a second that they were in any serious physical danger or that anything bad had happened to them. Most assumed that they were simply working on another cocoa farm nearby where the authorities would not see them. They could also be working in the city, or even be in school somewhere. Nobody knows. Or at least nobody is saying. Fear of a ban on cocoa exports has made producers expert at keeping children out of sight. But little progress has been made in tackling the underlying causes of child labour.

Heart of the industry

I didn't meet Alhassan's employer. But it is not hard to understand why they hired him. Producing cocoa is hard work. Many hands are needed to pluck pods, weed soil, prune trees and carry beans. It is a difficult job for one person to do alone.

About 90 to 95 per cent of the world's cocoa is produced by smallholder farmers on plantations roughly 3 hectares in size.[16] On most the production per hectare is either low or very low. In many cases, yields have been stagnant for some time. Roughly one-third of farms yield as little as 137.5 kg per hectare.[17] What this means is that the poorest farmers can make just $500 a year, an income which makes it impossible to do little more than survive, let alone hire labourers, buy fertiliser or invest in new seedlings. In this scenario, it is not difficult to understand why smallholders choose to use the cheapest labour they can find, often their own families.

Producers are not just vulnerable to falls in price but also to changes in circumstance. A bereavement or illness can leave them struggling for cash. Caring for his dying mother cost Paul Armah his farm. With no money to pay for the hospital bills or the funeral, the Betenase farmer borrowed 2 million old cedis from a moneylender. He was charged 100 per cent interest. Within six months he had lost his holding. His story is by no means unusual, said village chief Nana Kwaku Donkor. Many do not have bank accounts and rely on loan sharks instead. This can have devastating consequences. At that time, Nana Kwaku Donkor had ten cases of unpaid debt to adjudicate on. The penalty for non-payment can be steep, he said. 'If you have any asset, they will take the asset in place of the loan or take your cocoa farm for ten years and then give it back to you', he said.

In this kind of hand-to-mouth existence, family labour holds cocoa enterprises together. Without it, smallholders would struggle to harvest the crop. Most simply don't earn enough to hire other people to do it. I met a few farmers, who were honest enough to complain about the difficulty of running their holdings because of the crackdown on child labour. One chief executive of a European cocoa company admitted: 'The only way it works and something the chocolate manufacturers will never tell you ever ... they do all know the truth, they just don't say it – if you didn't get families with free labour, it doesn't work.'

The success of the cocoa industry hinges on the availability of families, those of the farm owner or caretaker, to harvest the crop. This sector, the IITA survey found, is one 'with stagnant technology, low yields, and an increasing demand for unskilled workers trapped in a circle of poverty'. As long as producers run their smallholdings in such a hand-to-mouth fashion, there will always be at least some children working on cocoa farms. This is a complex problem, one which has stumped the most well-meaning activists. Progress on the Harkin–Engel protocol has been slow. After a string of delays, industry plans to have an independently verified certification programme in place by the end of 2010.[18] There are a clutch of different industry-funded initiatives. As of June 2008, industry and individual companies had provided nearly $10 million to the International Cocoa Initiative, which works with communities in Ghana and Côte d'Ivoire.[19] At the same time, some 30,000 farmers across West Africa have been on industry-funded training courses, a small proportion of the region's 2 million farmers.[20] Another 65,000 or so have been taught by other producers. Less than 5 per cent of children surveyed have knowingly participated in a government or industry project, the Tulane University report found. There is some indication that child labour on cocoa farms is falling, it said, a drop which could be attributed to a decline in the crop in Côte d'Ivoire, publicity about child labour or a rise in living standards in both countries.

Senator Harkin wants industry to commit more money to eradicating child labour. He wants chocolate companies to invest roughly $20 million a year. Donor governments, he said, could also step up to the plate, and the Ivorian and Ghanaian governments should pressure cocoa buyers to help them. 'It doesn't mean that overnight everything changes', he said. 'It means that in the next year or two or three, we can begin to see pretty dramatic changes in those countries, as long as they don't back off.'

At the same time, activists have consistently called on chocolate companies to pay more for their cocoa. 'If they had enough wherewithal to hire and bring in adult workers, they would do it', said Bama Athreya of the International Labor Rights Fund. But a simple price increase might not deliver the desired benefits. For a start, the amount of cash farmers receive in their hand depends on the taxation levied by government. A price rise also means little to a producer who harvests just two bags a year. For him or her, a 10 per cent price rise can mean just $30. This is welcome, but hardly life-changing. Without access to local banks, the extra money he receives might disappear into the hands of a loan shark or he might have to split it with a caretaker. This is an economic issue but not one that can be resolved by simply writing a cheque.

Decades of political mismanagement, theft and waste mean that large parts of rural Ghana and Côte d'Ivoire are massively underdeveloped. Smallholdings, poor education and low yields conspire to keep farmers stuck in a trap of low returns.

Often, the only way cocoa can make economic sense for these producers is for whole families, their own or a caretaker's, to be involved on the farm. I felt the problem of child labour could not be tackled by well-meaning or misguided consumer campaigns. I began to think that if you wanted to get children off cocoa farms, then it was the business of cocoa farming itself that needed to be addressed. What needs to change is the way in which farmers produce the beans for the world's favourite sweet.

FOUR

FOLLOW THE MONEY

The man who couldn't keep a secret

It was midnight in Paris when Osange Silou Kieffer answered the phone. 'Your husband has been kidnapped', the caller said, and hung up. This must be a joke, she thought, a sick joke. Osange lived in Paris and was separated from Guy André Kieffer, a journalist. The 54-year-old lived in Abidjan, Côte d'Ivoire, where he wrote about politics, corruption and cocoa. The world's biggest cocoa producer, the country whose beans are found in nearly every chocolate bar, earned more than $2 billion from the crop each year.[1] Yet farmers had little to show for it. Many questioned what was happening to Côte d'Ivoire's billions of cocoa taxes. Rumours and allegations swirled around the Ivorian press and the industry. An agronomist by training, the French-Canadian reporter wanted to find out more. Osange, originally from Guadaloupe, knew that Guy André was a campaigning journalist who cared passionately about what he did. But that night in Paris she had no idea quite how much trouble he was in. The next day, 17 April 2004, a Saturday, she tried to call Guy André. His phone was switched off. She tried again, to no avail. Later she called his friends. They told her the same as the midnight caller. This was no joke. Guy André had been kidnapped.[2]

Left wing and idealistic, Guy André had gone to Abidjan on a mission. As a child, he had always had a book in his hand. As an adult, his Paris apartment was jammed with papers. He was, his brother said, a bank of facts about economics and international affairs. For eighteen years, he had written about commodities for *La Tribune*, the French economic daily. Côte d'Ivoire and its cocoa riches fascinated him. These beans fed factories around the world and could be found in nearly every bar of chocolate on every supermarket shelf. Yet farmers remained poor. He wanted to know why. In 2002, disillusioned with his life and work in Paris, he took a job in Abidjan at a consultancy which had won a contract to audit the cocoa sector. Osange had known him since their student days together in Canada. She had a daughter, Canelle, with him. She knew why he wanted to do it. 'I understood him as someone interested in justice, who wanted to revolutionise the sector. I understood he needed to do it.'

At first glance, Abidjan appears to be a very pleasant place to live. Since independence, the relationship between President Houphouet Boigny and successive French administrations had been a close one. The biggest French companies were invested there.[3] For thousands of French people, Abidjan provided a comfortable home in a tropical climate. If you turned on a tap, water would run freely. If you switched on a light, it would flicker into brightness without recourse to a generator. During the day, polished European cars glide into the business district of the Plateau, where high-rise offices overlook a lagoon. At night, restaurants serve fine French food and doormen usher well-heeled residents into Western hotels. Many called the Ivorian capital the Paris of Africa.

But there was another side to Côte d'Ivoire, one which made Osange wary about the trip that Guy André was about to make.

In this other Côte d'Ivoire, rubbish was piled high on the streets and children knocked on the dark windows of four-wheel-drives, looking for coins. This country was one where migrants disappeared, never to be seen again, money vanished from government bank accounts, and no one liked it when a journalist asked too many questions. Osange felt Côte d'Ivoire was a place of secrets. She worried how the straight-talking journalist would fare. The man she knew frequently breached confidences. 'He cannot keep anything to himself. He does not really believe that anything is off the record; he considers keeping information to himself as contrary to being a journalist', she said. 'Guy André did not have a sense of limits; someone like that cannot live in a country like that.'

In the months and years that followed, Osange was proved right. Someone like Guy André could not live in Côte d'Ivoire. Five years after Osange received that phone call in Paris, mentioning his name in Côte d'Ivoire is one of the quickest ways to change the tone of a conversation. 'You should be careful, you know what happened to Guy André', an embassy official in Abidjan said. An industry source said: 'Writing about cocoa can be dangerous. You do know about Guy André?' An NGO worker in Bouake froze when I said I was writing about the crop. He said he felt nervous because 'of what happened to Kieffer'. Guy André was not the only journalist in Abidjan to write about corruption and politics. The front pages of the local press are scattered with accusations of wrongdoing and hints of innuendo. Nor did he write simply about cocoa. But, in the years since his disappearance, his name has become a potent symbol for much of what is wrong in the cocoa sector. The shadow of Guy André looms large over those eager to campaign for justice for producers. For many in Côte d'Ivoire, the French-Canadian journalist symbolises the fact that it is best not to ask too many questions about cocoa money.

The new president

The Kieffers not only knew Côte d'Ivoire well, they also knew Laurent Gbagbo, the country's president, personally. They had met him in the 1980s when he lived in exile in Paris. There Gbagbo worked as a Spanish teacher while at night he edited a book on democracy in Côte d'Ivoire.[4] As one of the first politicians to challenge openly the French-backed regime of President Felix Houphouet Boigny, Gbagbo had been jailed for 'subversive teaching' in the early 1970s.[5] The man the Kieffers knew in Paris was left wing and progressive. He was eager to bring democracy to his country. But many in Côte d'Ivoire were angry at Gbagbo's success in the 2000 election. They felt he had stolen victory in a poll which Alassane Ouattara, one of his main rivals, had been ineligible to contest. In spite of the reports from Abidjan, Osange still had faith in Gbagbo. 'We had known him for years, we supported him. ... I really believed that Gbagbo would move to democracy, that the politics would change; he [Guy André] had the same hope,' she said. 'As I knew him [Gbagbo] I really thought it would happen.'

Guy André wanted to see how Côte d'Ivoire was faring under the new presidency. At that time, there were huge changes afoot in the cocoa industry. The reporter, a specialist in commodities, was keen to investigate. Gbagbo had become president at a crucial juncture in the history of the Ivorian cocoa trade. Since independence, the Caistab, a government stabilisation fund, had set a minimum farm-gate price and managed exports. This system allowed bureaucrats and politicians in Abidjan to cream off cash at the expense of producers. 'When you have a major actor who can decide the quantity they are going to sell, who they will sell it to and how they are going to sell it, of course it is corrupt', one industry official told me. The current system simply didn't work in the farmers' interest, John McIntire, the World Bank's economist in Côte d'Ivoire, told an industry dinner in 1999. Abolition of the Caistab would not only enrich smallholders, but would give a clear signal that it was no longer 'business as usual' in Côte d'Ivoire, he added.[6] But resistance to reform was ferocious. An early attempt to introduce an electronic bidding system was sabotaged.[7] Many in the local elite were profiting from the status quo. They did not want the system to change. A government minister went so far as to say that if the Bank 'mess[ed] with cocoa, there will be blood on the streets'.[8] World Bank officials continued to push for change. They were convinced reform would improve producers' lives.

Côte d'Ivoire had a weak negotiating hand in these discussions. It was heavily in debt and needed help from the same institutions that wanted it to overhaul the sector. It finally capitulated to pressure and agreed to reform in exchange for debt relief. Under this plan, the Caistab was to be abolished and farmers would no longer receive a minimum price for their cocoa. They would instead negotiate terms with buyers. This was the biggest change to the sector since independence. Cocoa and the use of cocoa money had been an important part of how Côte d'Ivoire had been run and managed since independence. Boigny's ability and willingness to use cocoa money to reward the faithful, curry support and smooth over cracks had kept the country ticking over. These were big changes, aimed at improving the incomes and lives of farmers. Hopes were high.

But liberalisation did not proceed according to plan. The abolition of the Caistab coincided with the overthrow of President Bédié in late 1999. The new government, led by President Robert Guei, created two new bodies to regulate the cocoa trade. When Gbagbo took power after an election later that year, he set up another three. At the time of liberalisation, a World Bank official told me, Gbagbo, then in opposition, had told him reform made

sense. But the government later realised cocoa could provide a
valuable source of finance, he said, hence the creation of these
new institutions. These bodies had not been part of the World
Bank blueprint, but, with hindsight at least, their establishment
did not surprise analysts. 'The only way they knew to govern
was by handing out the cocoa money', one reporter present in
Abidjan at the time said. 'I don't think the style of government
they had had since independence could have been maintained
without having huge and unaccountable access to cocoa [funds].
That is why they reinstituted it by other means.'

The government quickly appointed its allies to important
positions in the cocoa business. At the same time, it introduced
new levies on cocoa and coffee to fund these bodies. By January
2003, exporters were paying 27 cents of levies on each kilogram
of cocoa, nine times as much as they had paid in 1999.[9] This had
a direct impact on the money that farmers received. The more
taxes exporters paid, the less they gave producers for their cocoa.
In addition to these levies, cocoa taxes also rose from 26 cents in
1999 to 70 cents in 2003.[10] Introduction of the liberalised system
had coincided with a drop in international prices. No longer
protected by a minimum price, smallholder income fell.

Very little of the money raised from these taxes was spent on
supporting the farmer. In contrast, the men and women who
ran these organisations were well paid for their efforts. In 2001
alone, board members of one cocoa body held fifty-seven board
meetings. They received up to 3.3m CFA each to attend every
meeting.[11] At one stage the head of the Bourse du Café et Cacao
(BCC) earned an average of £31,000 a month.[12] These executives
became used to a high standard of living, one funded by the
cocoa farmer. Once when an executive went to London to meet
with cocoa industry representatives, he flew into a rage when he
found that the Ivorian delegation had been booked to stay at the

Hilton, not the Berners Hotel. To an outsider, these are both top-end London hotels. But angered by the change, he flew to Paris instead.[13]

This was the world Guy André entered when he came to Abidjan in January 2002. Within the industry, it was widely alleged that the new government was trying to share out the cocoa spoils with people from the west of Côte d'Ivoire, the Bete. These were people who had sold or leased their land to migrants from elsewhere. They felt they had not benefited from all that Côte d'Ivoire had to offer. At the same time, large American companies such as ADM and Cargill were building their operations in Abidjan. The sector was in flux. Guy André, an expert in commodities and a supporter of Gbagbo, wanted to lift the veil on what one commentator called the 'dark, confused world' of cocoa.[14]

An avenging journalist

The Côte d'Ivoire in which Guy André lived and worked was one where many people lived off the proceeds of cocoa money. This became clear when in January 2002 he started to work for Commodities Corporate Consulting (CCC), the company tasked to audit the sector. As he and his colleagues unearthed information about the use of farmers' cash, his journalistic instincts took over. He began to write stories under a pseudonym for the local press, leaking information he received as part of his consultancy work, information that he believed should be in the public domain; 'Things he should have kept to himself, things which stank of corruption', said Osange. This was a dangerous game to play. A journalist's prime motivation is to publish information. Guy André had been hired to be a consultant, not a reporter, but he remained 'an avenging journalist' by night. His actions were destined to annoy those in power.

As stories surfaced in Ivorian newspapers, Paul Antoine Bohoun Bouabré, the finance minister, began to believe that Guy André was running a campaign against him and other Ivorian cocoa officials.[15] CCC lost the contract to audit the cocoa sector. But Guy André decided to stay in Abidjan. He began reporting for *La Lettre du Continent*, the well-respected Paris newsletter, and local newspapers in Abidjan. At that time, Côte d'Ivoire was in upheaval. As civil war erupted, life in the capital and around the country quickly deteriorated. Ivorian newspapers accused the French of backing the rebellion, of favouring Ouattara and of failing to rescue Côte d'Ivoire from attack. In Abidjan, a youth militia, known as the Jeune Patriotes, frequently took to the streets of the capital, attacking immigrants and northerners. For the French residents used to the ease and comfort of the Paris of Africa, life changed dramatically. One minute you could be enjoying lobster on the beach, the next you would be showing your passport to a young militia member at a hastily thrown up roadblock.

President Gbagbo was determined to see off the rebels, but to do this he needed money. He called for donations to raise cash for ammunition, vehicles and aircraft to fight the insurgents. His allies in the industry stepped forward. On national television, in 2002, Henri Amouzou, the head of the FDPCC, a cocoa institution, presented cheques worth $20.5 million to the president for the war effort.[16] Others followed suit. These bodies were funded by cocoa taxes. The money they raised was meant to help the farmer, but these contributions made clear that this money was theirs to do what they wanted with, even wage war. A European Commission audit in 2005 found that money was being transferred to the president's office from quasi-fiscal agencies.[17] Set up to help the farmer, these bodies increasingly 'seem to pursue their own interests', found a UN panel of experts report from the same year.[18]

Many cocoa businesses felt under pressure to support the war effort. Local radio stations delivered daily updates on who had made donations. Those who hadn't given money could be accused of supporting the uprising. 'They [the government] were accusing us of supporting the rebels because a guy sitting on the Board was from the north', said one executive at a multinational, nervous about being interviewed in his office in the port area of Vridi in Abidjan. He and other exporters deny making donations to the war effort but made clear that they were walking a tricky line: 'Lets face the realities [*sic*], it was a difficult situation for everybody. The easiest thing is to accuse, to have your competitor say [that you support the rebels], then you have security forces on your back... You have to be careful.' Their priority was, at all costs, to get the beans. What could they do, he asked, ignore the government? 'At the end of the day, what do you do? Abandon all your investments here, say goodbye guys, we will come back another day?'

It was an open secret that cocoa taxes, in theory collected to help the farmer, were being used to buy arms. Where else would Côte d'Ivoire get the money from, Appia Kabran, a pro-Gbagbo politician, asked me. 'The country is attacked. The cocoa money belongs to the Ivorians, not the World Bank. We are too polite. This is our money, we can spend it how we want. Why do you ask us about our money?' he asked. For some, the payouts were just reward for all that Gbagbo had done for his people. Lucien Tapé Doh, the BCC chairman, said: 'When people say we gave money to Gbagbo. It is true. So what? It is him who gave us the sector.'[19]

Cocoa taxes also became a vital source of revenue for the rebels in northern Côte d'Ivoire. When war broke out, the government in Abidjan stopped all shipments north, including medication, and cut all funding. Teachers and other government employees fled.[20] The north of Côte d'Ivoire has long been poorer than the south. Its farmers mostly rely on the sale of cotton to make ends meet.[21] In sharp contrast to Abidjan, Bouake is low-rise and dilapidated. Water often runs out, there are frequent power cuts and the city's roads are pockmarked and battered. As the war intensified, farmers in the north, which produces about 10 per cent of the Ivorian crop,[22] decided not to send their beans to Abidjan. They chose instead to send them overland to the port of Lomé in Togo. For a canny businessman, this made economic sense. Government taxes were high. The rebels demanded a fee, but one far lower than that demanded by the Abidjan administration. At one stage, at least three international companies were believed to be buying cocoa in the north.[23]

This illicit trade provided a useful source of cash for the rebels. By one estimate, they earned as much as $30 million a year from this activity.[24] The crop is considered to be the single biggest source of revenue for the Forces Nouvelles.[25]

This money was used to pay troops a minimal salary, the *prime du savon*, or the price of soap. But as hospitals, roads and schools fell into disrepair, many in the north became cynical of the rebels' intentions. People in Boauke could see the rebels living in hotels, buying large vehicles and building big houses. Guillaume Soro, their leader, sped through the city in a blue Mercedes and a convoy of armed vehicles.[26] One resident told me: 'They were making money and the people were getting poorer. They just came to make money.' Just as in the south of Côte d'Ivoire, the proceeds of cocoa were being used to fund the war and line the pockets of the people in power. These beans provided a lifeline for the millions of people reliant on the sale of cocoa to survive. Global chocolate companies needed them to keep their multi-billion-dollar businesses ticking over. During this brief war, thousands were killed and many more displaced. But as long as the beans kept coming, few questions were asked.

A reporter in danger

It became increasingly dangerous to be a reporter in Côte d'Ivoire. For decades, many foreign journalists had lived in Abidjan, using it as a base from which to cover the region. Fighting had stopped in 2003, but the country remained split in two. Many felt that Côte d'Ivoire was no longer a safe place to live and work. In 2003, Jean Hélène, a reporter for Radio France Internationale, had been shot dead by a police officer as he went to interview some opposition supporters. Reuters and AP, the large news agencies, moved their regional offices from Abidjan to Dakar in nearby Senegal. From then on, the big agencies mostly hired local correspondents to cover Ivorian news and politics. Guy André was one of the few foreign correspondents remaining in Côte d'Ivoire.

Guy André continued to write for *La Lettre du Continent* and other Ivorian newspapers. He wrote about the planned exchange of cocoa for helicopters, the transfer of state funds to Guinea Bissau and the operations of BNI, a state bank.[27] His writing rattled many in Côte d'Ivoire. Michel Legré, Simone Gbagbo's brother-in-law, later said: 'Every time Guy Andre published a critical article, I went to see my friends in power to say to them, yes, he has written this, but you can always ... meet with him to discuss it.'[28]

Guy André was treading a dangerous line. He frequently got facts wrong. While the articles he wrote for *La Lettre du Continent* were checked and edited, the same reports appeared unchanged in local newspapers, where he used a well-known pseudonym. Some questioned if he was using his journalism to settle business scores. At *La Tribune* he had been reined in by editors. Friends speculated that in Côte d'Ivoire he had lost his moorings, that he was adrift without a professional compass to guide him. 'If you don't stick to iron-clad rules, you get lost', one acquaintance said.

'You are no longer perceived as a journalist, if you start to tamper with rules; people can see you as a spy, and a business person.' Not only did his writing attract attention, so too did Guy André himself. Frequently short of money, he was loud and gregarious, always on his mobile phone, often shouting. He seemed to have taken on the role of crusader. He behaved, his brother said, like Zorro without the mask. He saw himself in the mould of Michael Moore, the American documentary maker, one colleague said. 'In Abidjan, that is suicide', he said. In a country at war, he was, the colleague added in French, an elephant in a porcelain shop.

Guy André also felt afraid. He knew that Paul Antoine Bohoun Bouabré, the finance minister, had twice asked the Council of Ministers to expel him from the country. But he also knew that the president had refused that request both times. Deep down, Guy André felt that, no matter what he wrote, the Gbagbo he knew in Paris might still look out for him. He felt that his articles kept the president's allies and enemies on their toes, and that the president liked this. He felt, Osange said, that the president would protect him. But people were running out of patience with Guy André.

In early 2004, Guy André began to receive threats. He became jumpy and nervous. It was difficult to spend an evening with him, one acquaintance said. He was always on his mobile phone, always changing arrangements at the last minute, always looking to move somewhere else. On 13 April 2004, he called the offices of *La Lettre du Continent* in Paris. He was nervous and anxious.[29] It had become dangerous for him in Côte d'Ivoire, he said. He was going to take some time out. Three days later, Guy André met Michel Legré, his friend and Simone Gbagbo's brother-in-law, in the car park of a shopping centre in Abidjan.[30] Legré said that Guy André then left to go to Ghana. Shortly afterwards, his phone went dead. No one has seen him since.

Abduction

Rumours spread quickly through the Ivorian capital. Newspaper reports suggested that Guy André had been abducted by an army commando from the supermarket car park. Staff on duty that day told reporters they had seen nothing.[31] Many people were too afraid to talk. If a white journalist could disappear in central Abidjan in broad daylight, was anyone safe? Rita, Guy André's Ghanaian girlfriend, fled to her home country the weekend of his disappearance, fearing for her life. In Paris, Osange called everyone she knew who might be able to help. She was separated from Guy André but they remained in touch, not least because they had a daughter together, Canelle. Bernard Kieffer, who knew that his brother took frequent trips to Ghana to escape the pressure of Abidjan, wondered if Guy André had arranged his own temporary disappearance.

Within days, Osange decided to travel to the Ivorian capital with Guy André's brothers. They met President Gbagbo, who reassured them he would do what he could to find the missing journalist. At the same time, it became clear to Guy André's family that not only had the president been keeping a close eye on him but some of the journalist's close acquaintances had not been straight in their dealings with him. One told Osange he had shared details of the reporter's investigations with the president's office. Guy André had known and approved, he claimed, something which Osange found impossible to believe. Others said that Guy André's phone was being tapped. The local press reported that a white man's body had been found in a suburb in Abidjan, but that this body had later disappeared.

Guy André had dual citizenship and the reporter's family visited the French and Canadian embassies in search of help and answers. As they trawled around the city, Bernard frequently felt that people were trying to deflect them from the truth, whatever that could be. The French embassy advised them to hire a detective, he said, a suggestion he found ludicrous given that the strong presence of the French army meant they had the equipment, resources and expertise needed to help find a missing French citizen. At the same time, diplomats told those who asked that Guy André had been involved in something shady. Guy André was not just a journalist, he had other business interests, they said. But people who knew him doubt that he had any motivation other than seeking the truth. 'He was incapable of earning money except as a journalist or a consultant', his brother said. 'He was an intellectual and not a man of money.' He may have done consultancy work, one former colleague said, but he certainly wasn't shipping cocoa, implying he had neither the resources nor the motivation. The Kieffers felt that the French authorities were shying away from helping them. Paris was wary of what their enquiries would mean for already fraught Franco-Ivorian relationships. It didn't want to further muddy troubled waters with its former colony. It was clear that Guy André had disappeared, his brother said, at the wrong time and in the wrong place.

In the weeks that followed, Guy André's laptop was found in the house of Michel Legré, Simone Gbagbo's brother-in-law and the last person to see Guy André alive. Osange had never known Guy André to part with his laptop, had never known him even to allow Canelle, his daughter, to touch it. She could not conceive of how it could innocently end up in the house of Legré. Later, Guy André's car was found at the airport.[32] In an interview with French investigators, Legré blamed President Gbagbo's advisers for Guy André's disappearance. He later retracted those statements. Neither Simone Gbagbo nor her husband are suspected of being directly linked with his disappearance. For her part, Mrs Gbagbo has vociferously denied any involvement.[33]

Bits of information continued to emerge, all supporting the theory that Guy André had been kidnapped. A man named Berte Seydou told French television[34] that he was a driver in the commando unit which had abducted Kieffer from the supermarket car park. Kieffer had spent thirty minutes in a villa outside Abidjan, before being taken to the presidency, where he spent two days and two nights, Seydou said. He was later taken to a farm, where he was killed, he alleged. Still no body had been found. Jean Tony Oulai, the alleged leader of the group who kidnapped him, is in custody in France.

As part of his inquiries, Judge Patrick Ramaël, the judge leading the French investigation, interviewed Madame Gbagbo in Abidjan.[35] Raymond Tschimou, the prosecutor leading the Ivorian inquiry, blamed Guy André's French colleagues at CCC, the commodity consultancy, for his disappearance. Tschimou alleged that Guy André was blackmailing them because they were laundering money,[36] claims CCC denied. Guy André's family view these accusations as a red herring.

Relationships between France and its former colony remain volatile. In Abidjan in 2008, I sought an interview with Raymond Tschimou. I was ushered into his office by an aide who had misunderstood my request. Once Mr Tschimou realised I was a journalist, he told me he was too busy to speak. He had previously spoken to reporters but had no desire to discuss Guy André. This case is simply too 'hot, hot, hot', my driver and colleague told me. President Sarkozy told Guy André's family that the situation between the countries cannot normalise until this affair is resolved. This statement implies a greater level of political engagement than has in fact taken place. In practice, political intervention has been timid, episodic and 'not really effective', Bernard, Guy André's brother, said.

Osange still visits Abidjan, desperate to keep the search for justice alive. Many believe that Guy André, who had heart problems, was the victim of a beating which went wrong.

'I rather think he had colliding business interests; he was to be taught a lesson and it went wrong', one said. Without a body, no one knows. Whether or not government officials played any part in what happened, Bernard Kieffer said, they have certainly not helped the investigation. In early 2009, the family made a renewed appeal for witnesses. No one came forward, which is strange in a city where gossip and political rumours crackle and spread like fire. Those who ordered his disappearance cast a long shadow, dark enough to keep those who know something away from police stations and French investigators. Other than Osange and Guy André's family and friends, it is not clear who, if anyone, wants Guy André's mysterious abductors brought to justice.

Business as usual

Since Guy André's disappearance, the discredited cocoa institutions have been abolished, and their managers thrown in jail after widespread allegations of corruption. Under pressure from the World Bank and the IMF, Côte d'Ivoire has cut levies. But while deeper reform of the cocoa sector is promised, progress has been slow.[37] Meaningful change is unlikely before an election. In the meantime, farmers continue to harvest cocoa, exporters continue to ship it and government continues to tax it. There have been frequent calls for greater transparency. Global Witness, a campaign group, wants to know what multinationals pay the government and what the government does with that money. Without detailed information on the use of cocoa revenues, campaigners argue, it is difficult for real change to take place. At the same time, American federal investigators want to find out what happened to Ivorian funds invested in a chocolate factory in Fulton, amid fears it was used to launder cash.[38] The United Nations panel of experts has complained of the difficulty of getting meetings with, let alone information about cocoa finances from, the government.[39]

Industry has declined to make details of payments to the Ivorian government public. It is up to the Ivorians what they spend their money on, sources say repeatedly. 'I am not trying to run Ivory Coast, I am just a businessman, fair and simple', one industry official told me. 'If they don't want me there, I would leave; if I can't make any money, I will leave as well. We are really simple people; we are not going to go down the line of making moral issues in every country in the world.' The chocolate industry's job, said Phil Sigley of the Federation of Cocoa Commerce, an industry lobby group, is simply to buy the beans. If it didn't, millions of people in Côte d'Ivoire, north and south, would go hungry. 'Even if you could trace cocoa, would you want to stop the wheels turning, if there are political moves to try to bring peace to the country?', he asked. 'These issues are to do with political leadership. At no time has anyone said [we should] interfere with that supply chain.' Illicit shipments in northern Côte d'Ivoire are acknowledged at the highest levels of government, the industry official – believed to have been involved in the trade – told me.

> I think everyone in government is fully aware of what is going on, since you have Soro and Gbagbo working together. There needs to be some income for these people in the north, the leaders, and this is a very good way of doing it. I am sure there would be ways to stop it. I think they don't want to stop it; it suits everybody.

But there are moral and business risks inherent in this hands-off stance. Is it really enough to turn a blind eye to whatever abuses of power are taking place? Is it acceptable for businesses to buy beans from whomever will sell them, no matter what the proceeds are used for?

If farmers continue to feel cheated, output in Côte d'Ivoire, already stagnant, could drop. High taxation is already pushing farmers to plant other crops. 'The most fundamental reason [for stagnant production] is the high levels of taxation in [Côte d'Ivoire]. This has given to farmers a lot of incentive to switch to other products', said ICCO's Jan Vingerhoets. 'There is no incentive to work on the long-term maintenance of the farms. A farmer has to work continuously on rehabilitation. If he starts neglecting the farm ... then it goes down. There is little use of fertilisers, little use of pesticides.'

It is not hard to understand the extreme sensitivity of these questions. Cocoa cash is intricately interwoven with the political situation in Côte d'Ivoire, north and south. This cash is vitally important to President Gbagbo. 'He is also fighting to survive. Are the farmers high on the list? Not really, because they won't really cause him any trouble', one official said. His priority is clinging on to power, another told me. 'He will leave that place in a coffin.'

Several organisations have tried to follow in Guy André's footsteps, eager to find out what is happening to Côte d'Ivoire's cocoa cash. His disappearance illustrates the dangers of trying to shed light on where the money goes. Unpicking the cocoa cash trail lays bare the web of political and personal connections that pin Gbagbo's administration together. It makes clear how little producers get for their work and how little their representatives deliver. Checking the cocoa cash involves more than simply counting the beans. It is also an integral part of any lasting political agreement. 'Cocoa is part of the problem', one analyst told me. 'It has to be part of the solution.'

FIVE

FROM BEAN TO BAR

In 1978, at the age of 16, Steve Wallace volunteered for a student home-stay programme. The American teenager was eager to ex-perience life away from his home state of Wisconsin and chose Ghana, a country he knew little about. He went to stay with the family of Yaw Brobby, a businessman in Sunyani, a small, neat town in the country's north-west. There he was welcomed by Brobby, his three wives and twenty-one children.

Brobby was a shopkeeper but, to Wallace's surprise, the shelves in his store were virtually empty. Held together by the money it earned from cocoa, Ghana had very little foreign exchange. Hardly anything was being imported. The family had electricity for a few hours every day and running water every third day or so. There were no phones and it took three or four weeks for letters to arrive. Life in Sunyani was in sharp contrast to the lakes, snow and privilege of his home state. Wallace was entranced. When his stay ended, he was determined to return.

Almost thirty years later, I met him on one of his many return visits to Ghana. The country we meet in is very different to the one he knew then. His accommodation is one of several Western-style hotels in Accra. Its bar is stocked with beer, wines and whiskys. Its menu offers burgers, fries and pasta, as well as Ghanaian dishes such as banku and tilapia. New buildings are going up everywhere in Accra. Many people have mobile phones, often more than one. There are still power cuts, partly because demand is rising far faster than the decrepit grid can cope with. This is a vastly different country to the one Wallace visited in 1978. But his first trip left a deep and lasting impression. 'It was probably the seminal formative experience of my life, without question', he said, wonder creeping into his voice as he talks about his stay. 'It is that wonderful book that is in the bookshop that you keep going back to every year and flipping open.... Almost everything I saw challenged some piece of what I had grown up with, from family interactions to schooling.'

After that summer visit, Steve Wallace went to college and became a tax lawyer. During his studies, he wondered if and how he could return to Ghana. He considered joining the foreign service or working for a charity which would post him in West Africa. Remembering the empty shop shelves and the lack of imports, he wondered if it wouldn't be more useful to set up a business, one that would bring in foreign exchange. He lacked the money or expertise to invest in Ghana's gold, bauxite or diamonds. But he knew the country was one of the world's biggest suppliers of cocoa. These beans were made into chocolate by Mars, Hershey and Cadbury's at their factories in Europe and the USA. Wallace wondered if it would be possible to turn some of that cocoa into chocolate in Ghana. The country made hundreds of millions of dollars every year from the beans. But the market for cocoa products and chocolate was far more valuable, worth an estimated $75 billion. 'I didn't grow up eating a lot of chocolate', said Wallace, dressed in a suit and tie at a poolside bar in Accra. 'But it was a vehicle to get me back to Ghana. What I became intrigued with was adding value.'

For Wallace, the case for making chocolate in Ghana was clear. For every £1 bar, just seven pence is spent on cocoa ingredients, while 43 pence goes to the manufacturer.[1] Much of the value, or most of the profits, lies not in selling the beans to the chocolate company but in the process of turning the beans into a bar. At the same time, much of the price risk lies with the farmer. They are more vulnerable to volatile prices on commodity markets than large manufacturers, which are able to absorb such fluctuations more easily than a producer reliant on bean sales to survive.

There was another reason why Wallace wanted to add value, one which had nothing to do with financial gain and was also slightly more difficult to articulate. When people in the West think of gourmet food products, says Wallace, they think of European or American companies. Ask a chocolate lover what their favourite bar is, they will name Lindt, Cadbury or Mars. The world's chocolate is made far from West Africa, where most of the beans are sourced. Very little chocolate is made or eaten in the region itself. It is not a local food and does not feature in West African dishes. It is also beyond the price reach of many. Street children sell locally made bars, wrapped in a Kente-style paper, for 50 Ghanaian pesewas, or roughly 30 US cents, about twice as much as a street-side plate of rice. Wallace felt that value addition could change and deepen Westerners' perception of Africa. 'I wanted to demonstrate the very object lesson that gourmet food could come out of this continent', he said.

This perception of Africa as a provider of raw materials rather than finished goods reflects the fact that the continent has been left behind in the global march towards industrialisation. It produces few of the world's manufactured goods. In 2005, the world's manufacturing value-added totalled $6,536.6 billion, according to the United Nations Industrial Development Organization.[2] Of this $4,535.2 billion came from industrialised economies and

$1,892.5 billion from developing economies. Just $45.8 billion came from sub-Saharan Africa, an increase from $39.7 billion in 2000, but still a paltry figure. The contrast with parts of Asia is striking. East Asia and the Pacific accounted for $1146.7 billion in 2005, up from $770 billion in 2000.[3] 'The spectacular rise of the emerging economies, especially in East and South Asia, contrasts sharply with the industrial stagnation experienced by many middle-income countries and the continued industrial marginalisation of Africa and least developed countries elsewhere in the world', wrote Kandeh K. Yumkella, the director general of UNIDO, in 2009. Africa, it is clear, is being left behind.

This matters, and not just for reasons of national or regional pride. Wallace's belief in value addition is backed by some hard economic facts. Only in unusual circumstances, such as an extraordinary abundance of land or resources, have countries succeeded in developing without industrialising, noted UNIDO. In the case of East Asia, the impact of industrialisation has been explosive. Economies have been transformed in a matter of years. Industrialisation and value addition were central to Kwame Nkrumah's vision as to how the country should develop. But little progress has been made since Ghana won its independence. It has few factories of any description. More than fifty years after Nkrumah, nearly two-thirds of the world's cocoa beans come from West Africa,[4] but slightly less than one-fifth of those beans are ground on the continent.[5]

Today, the Omanhene Cocoa Bean company, owned by Wallace, makes, wraps and ships chocolate from Ghana, selling it in the USA and Japan. But the story of Omanhene, a Twi word which means 'paramount chief', is not a simple one of business success. Wallace's experience illustrates much of what is difficult about adding value in Africa and makes clear why other companies have been reluctant to follow in his path.

Recipe for success

Wallace was working in Washington when he started to look into making chocolate in Ghana. He dusted down library books and struck up conversations with pastry chefs and confectioners, asking them how to make the perfect chocolate bar. Creating a bar that remains cool on display and yet melts in your mouth is a mix of science and art. First, the cocoa beans are roasted. The slow heat releases a dark sweet smell and the shells are removed. The nibs, the inside of the beans, are then ground into a dark brown paste known as cocoa liquor. Some of this liquor is pressed to extract cocoa butter. The final chocolate mix, which contains cocoa liquor, sugar, milk and cocoa butter, is blended to a consistency where the particles of cocoa and sugar are too small for the tongue to detect. It is then repeatedly warmed and cooled. The finished bar should melt just below body temperature. Finally, it is moulded into a bar, wrapped and packed for sale.[6]

There are thousands of variations to this basic recipe. Manufacturers can add nuts, raisins, fudge and honeycomb. They can leave out the cocoa liquor and make white chocolate; they can leave out the milk and make dark chocolate; or they can blend the mix for longer to create the velvety taste associated with luxury chocolate. The taste, the colour and the mouth-feel or texture of the chocolate are determined by the precise proportion of ingredients and their processing. Subtle changes can make the difference between a bar that sells and one that flops.

The world's biggest chocolate companies were founded by entrepreneurs who mastered this process. Their names are still well known today: John Cadbury, who opened his first tea and coffee shop in Birmingham in 1824; Henri Nestlé, who developed a milk formula;[7] Rudolph Lindt, who created a machine to process cocoa;[8] Milton Hershey, who mastered a recipe for a sour milk chocolate for Americans; and Forrest Mars, the creator of the popular Mars bar.

Nearly two hundred years after John Cadbury opened his shop, the company he founded is the world's biggest chocolate company, thanks to its merger with Kraft in early 2010. In second place is Mars. Between them, Nestlé, Ferrero, Mars, Kraft and Cadbury Schweppes control more than half of the European market for consumer chocolate. This aggregate figure conceals a higher degree of concentration in specific national markets and for specific products. In the mid-1990s, for example, Cadbury, Mars and Nestlé accounted for approximately 75 per cent to 80 per cent of the UK chocolate confectionery market.[9]

These companies operate in the world's biggest markets, the same places that Wallace wanted to do business in. Europe and America account for more than 60 per cent of consumption.[10] But these markets are nearing maturity. If anything, Europeans and Americans might choose to eat less chocolate amid increased concerns about health and diet. Demand is, however, rising elsewhere. Eastern Europe now accounts for 12 per cent of global chocolate sales. While the average Chinese person eats just 200 grams of chocolate a year, this represents the tip of a burgeoning market. This is good news for European and Asian factories. Petra, an Indonesian company and Asia's largest cocoa processor, sells cheap chocolates, large and small, across the region.[11] It has a large and expanding market on its doorstep.

Africa and the Middle East, however, account for just 3 per cent of global sales. Very few Ghanaians or Ivorians eat chocolate. It is considered to be too expensive for a casual treat, and cocoa, a crop imported from South America, does not feature in West African dishes. Wallace wanted to make his chocolate for export. He wanted to prove that the kind of gourmet product that people associated with European and American food technology and taste could come from Africa. But he also had little choice in the matter: he had to export his chocolate. There was no local or regional market for his products.

If he was going to sell his wares in the USA, he needed to cater for American palates. Traditionally, Americans enjoyed a sweeter, more sugary chocolate than Europeans, who prefer a darker chocolate, made with more cocoa and less sugar. He decided to make a dark milk chocolate, a bar that would appeal to the American sweet tooth but would also have a strong cocoa flavour. He tinkered with the recipe, refined the maths in his head, the precise proportion of ingredients needed to get the taste he wanted. 'I gave a lot of mediocre chocolate to people at the beginning; it took a long time to get this production right', he said. After months of experiment, he had the recipe he wanted and the market in sight. But he was still some way from having the chocolate bar in his hand.

Millers and grinders

Once he had the recipe, Wallace needed to find a place in Ghana to make it. He had cashed in a life insurance policy to fund the business and he didn't have enough money to set up his own factory. In the early 1990s, his options were limited. Two factories, West African Mills and Cocoa Processing Company, processed cocoa in Ghana. On and off since independence, these two partly state-owned companies have ground beans into butter and paste. CPC makes small quantities of chocolate for sale locally. It has never seriously tried to sell these chalky, dry bars in the West. Wallace hoped that CPC would be able to make his chocolate for him.

But first he had to get the beans. Cocobod, the marketing board, controls sales and exports. Officials there were wary of him. 'This is a huge cultural, economic and political institution; the government of Ghana didn't want outsiders ... I could see they were protective', he said. After they agreed to supply him with beans, he then had to source milk and sugar from overseas – Ghana doesn't have a dairy industry – and find a company to wrap the finished chocolate bar. It also proved difficult to replicate the exact taste and flavour of the prototype bar created in the USA. He struggled to find a company able to provide the glossy wrap and finish that customers in the West wanted. Wallace became obsessed with getting it right. 'I became infatuated with this project. The biggest fear [I had] was I had lost all attachment to reality. Part of it is I was in too deep now [to stop]', he said. In 1994, four years after Wallace had first started looking at recipes, he sold his first chocolate bar.

Nearly fifteen years after Wallace started out, there are now far more cocoa factories in Ghana. Barry Callebaut opened a grinder in Ghana in 2001. ADM and Cargill have facilities there. These three companies are the world's biggest processors. In factories around the world, they grind cocoa into butter, powder and liquor, the building blocks of chocolate. Callebaut, the third-biggest processor,[12] is the biggest maker of industrial chocolate, the dark brown mix known as couverture.

These millers and grinders play an increasingly important role in the global chocolate industry. Barry Callebaut's website offers 1,650 recipes, everything from honey-flavoured to organic, mixing produce from Ghana, Côte d'Ivoire, Indonesia or Brazil to create different flavours. More and more companies actually outsource the manufacture of chocolate. This allows them to concentrate on advertising and marketing, doing everything they can to ensure that the hand that hovers over the sweet counter chooses their product. Cadbury sources some of its chocolate mix from Barry Callebaut, as does Hershey. On average, sweet companies source

11 per cent of their chocolate from companies such as these,[13] a figure which is expected to increase. The handful of companies that dominate this trade all now have factories in Ghana, where they grind the beans.

When President Kufuor took power in 2000, he encouraged these processors to set up in Ghana. There are numerous drawbacks to operating in West Africa. Factories located in Ghana are reliant on beans from one country only. This not only determines the flavour of the product; it also makes them vulnerable to crop failure or disease. Costs are high, not least because energy is expensive. While labour is cheap, automated food factories generally require few staff. Ghana is also far from the big consumer markets of Europe and America, where most of the world's chocolate is sold. It is more expensive to ship a cocoa product than it is to transport bags of beans. In order to persuade companies to set up factories in Ghana, Kufuor offered them cheaper beans and tax breaks. These inducements worked. Processors, hoping to secure supply by building factories locally, signed contracts. 'This will increase the benefits from the crop to the economy and, more importantly, reduce the dependence on the fickleness of the international commodity market', the then president said.[14]

But these factories, though impressive on paper, deliver Ghana little real advantage. Ghana now has enough capacity to process half its annual cocoa crop, but these factories mill beans – they do not make chocolate. Few jobs have been created at the largely automated facilities. Barry Callebaut employs just 100 people to process 60,000 tonnes of cocoa a year. The marketing board, which would prefer to export beans rather than sell them to local factories at a discount, frequently squabbles with processors about bean supply. It is not unusual for processors to run short of beans, a fact which irritates investors hugely. Some in Ghana also feel short-changed. Asked how Ghana has actually benefited from these deals, a Western manager at one of the plants told me that the best he could say is that at least 'it doesn't lose out'.

Hope Sona Ebai, the head of the Cocoa Producers' Alliance, summed up the realities of processing in West Africa: 'Some of these companies sell the story of value addition so well, they get tax breaks and other advantages, so at the end of the day the only impact on the local economy is the fifty to sixty jobs that are created; that is nothing compared to what they are really getting.' Others are equally dismissive of the advantages to government of local processing. 'What they [the government] would say is let's take a thirty-year view; at least we get some technology into the country. But I think that is nonsense. If they were building fighter jets, they would get some technology. A cocoa processing plant is reasonably sophisticated but it is not exactly rocket science', one industry official said.

Mars, Cadbury and Hershey have shown no interest in making the finished product in West Africa. It is difficult for them to get all the ingredients they need. It is far from the end consumer and an expensive place to do business. Chocolate is also an easily perishable sweet. Why, asked one Cadbury's official, would you make it in the Accra heat, ship it in air-conditioned freight so it can be sold in the rainy, temperate days of a UK summer?

For foreign investors, Africa is still playing catch-up with other, more attractive regions, which offer not just cheap labour but also a burgeoning consumer market. In the 1980s overvalued African currencies deterred industry from investing there. By the time the continent was reforming its economies – and devaluing its currencies – East Asia had established itself as an attractive location for business. Multinationals are more likely to set up in an already established region than blaze a trail in a new location.[15] Logistics are also hugely important. The ease with which you can move raw materials and finished products helps determine industrial competitiveness. Ghana ranks 125 out of 150 on UNIDO's global logistics performance index.[16] Behind this figure lies a real and serious issue. When I first met Wallace in 2007, he spoke of problems he was experiencing with shipping and electricity.

But for Wallace, unlike other manufacturers, the location was non-negotiable. He didn't just want to make any chocolate bar; he wanted to make chocolate in Ghana from Ghanaian cocoa beans. It was central to his motivation for going into business. Wallace struggled to get his chocolate made in Ghana. But he faced an even greater battle to get it on the shelves of supermarkets in the West.

Pricing the bar

The chocolate Wallace made in Ghana was never going to be cheap. Most of the bars made by the millers and grinders and the large chocolate companies sell for small change. If you go into a supermarket in the UK, you spend 60 pence on a Mars Bar, a Twix or Kit Kat. These companies have advantages that Wallace doesn't. As previously noted, increasingly brand names outsource chocolate manufacture to large groups with economies of scale and efficiency. These groups can operate just-in-time manufacturing, quickly sourcing raw materials when stocks run low, thus reducing their storage costs. It is difficult for Wallace, who buys raw materials from all over the world, to achieve that level of efficiency. 'I can't ever cut it that close. Things delay at customs. There could be a strike. Even in the US we have to carry a lot of inventory. Those things really cost us; the big companies can play those things like Tchaikovsky', he said.

Niche manufacturers can charge more for their products. The quality and exclusivity of Paul Young's work enables him to sell some of the UK's most expensive chocolate. Every day, he and his assistants take delivery of liquid chocolate from a premium chocolate company. They mix it with sugar, vanilla and occasionally soya lecithin, a natural emulsifier, and make the sweets which fill his shop in an exclusive part of North London. These truffles, ganaches and brownies lack preservatives, artificial flavourings, stabilisers, vegetable fat or glucose, all the ingredients that give supermarket chocolate its shelf life. These treats are expensive – he charges £3.50 for a 50 gram bar – but the appetite for these kinds of product is increasing.

More and more people perceive chocolate as a gourmet product. In the same way as wine connoisseurs talk of different grapes or vintages, chocolate experts talk about different aromas and flavours. These are completely different kinds of treat to a Mars Bar or Kit Kat. They usually carry a high cocoa content and a hefty price tag. Supermarket shelves are stacked with bars labelled 'premium', 'luxury' or 'continental'. They sell for as much as £1.99 apiece, three times more than the bars sold at the checkout. Nevertheless, in the UK, sales of premium chocolate, still a small part of the overall confectionary market, are rising.[17]

Are bars labelled as 'premium' really better chocolate? Chloe Doutre Roussel, a former chocolate buyer at Fortnum & Mason, picks apart the marketing rhetoric with gusto. Boasting about a high cocoa content is as ludicrous as praising a wine for its high alcohol content. 'Percentage is a meaningless concept; you need the right amount of sugar and cacao to allow expression of aromas, to allow it to bloom', she notes. Origin can make a difference, but simply buying Venezuelan beans does not guarantee a higher-quality chocolate bar, she added. In an industry dominated by smallholder plantations, the quality of the bean varies hugely within regions and within countries. Even the highest-quality bean can still result in a poor bar of chocolate. Some of this chocolate is wonderful, she said. But too often consumers were being gulled by clever marketing. Whether or not these bars are actually tastier or 'better' chocolate, the rise in demand for premium products has made it easier for a niche producer to charge more for their chocolate.

In designing his price structure, Wallace also had to consider import taxes in the USA and Japan, his chosen markets. Chocolate imports are generally charged as part of a complex tariff regime designed to protect sugar farmers. In Europe and the USA producers are guaranteed a price for their sugar which can be three times higher than the world market price. Manufacturers that use non-subsidised sugar pay additional taxes on their products. Under the African Growth and Opportunity Act (AGOA), one of the most high-profile US initiatives to promote trade with Africa, some goods can be exported duty-free to the USA. But it has made little difference to chocolate companies, Wallace said. In general, schemes such as AGOA can offer manufacturers an advantage, UNIDO said. But so far AGOA has not stimulated any new investment, especially in West Africa, the UNIDO report found.[18]

Wallace would face few taxes if he exported his chocolate to Europe. Ghana and Côte d'Ivoire have not been taxed on finished chocolate or cocoa products sold into the European Union since they signed Economic Partnership Agreements in 2007. But these deals were controversial. The two countries agreed to cut import taxes on European goods over fifteen years, depriving them of revenue and forcing their own industries to compete with cheaper imports. If they hadn't signed, they could have faced higher taxes on exports to the EU.

The details of the negotiations for the EPAs shed a light on how difficult it is to make chocolate in West Africa. No European chocolate or confectionary company opposed the abolition of taxes on chocolate made in West Africa, an official at the industry

lobbyist Caobisco told me. This chocolate was not a threat
to their business. There are so many factors working against
successful production in West Africa that no extra barrier or
tariff was needed to protect European industry from African
chocolate manufacturers. Tariff structures are only one part of
the export jigsaw, Wallace agreed. Several other obstacles stand
in his way.

The desire for chocolate that is more than just an empty treat,
chocolate that is seen as a gourmet product, chocolate that is
talked about in the same way that wine connoisseurs talk about
Bordeaux or Chardonnay, have pushed up the price for the right
product. A niche producer like Wallace needs to charge a high
price in order to make a profit. Wallace hoped that consumers
would be willing to pay extra for a story, be that story one of
exclusivity or quality. 'We have to be able to sell at a premium as
we don't enjoy the economies of scale against very large chocolate
firms. The world doesn't need another cheap chocolate bar; we
offer a different story and a different price point', he said. The
story that Wallace told was one of a chocolate bar made in Ghana,
the only one of its kind on supermarket shelves. All these things
mean that a niche producer like Wallace can sell his chocolate at
a high price. Wallace's Omanhene bar is on the more expensive
end of the shelf, at around $4 for a 100 gram bar.

On the shelf

It took Wallace a long time to get to the stage where he had a bar
of chocolate to sell. He had to develop a recipe, get the ingredients
to Ghana, perfect production, wrap the bar, negotiate tariffs
and pricing. All this was tough enough. But these challenges
were dwarfed by the hardest one of all: getting his chocolate on
the supermarket shelf. Like many small manufacturers, Wallace

initially thought that sales would spread by word of mouth, that fans of his chocolate would ask retailers to stock the bars, that slowly demand would increase and with it his bottom line. The reality proved to be more complicated. 'I tell people jokingly, but I actually think it is quite true, you can have chocolate, go to a major retailer and say it is free, put it on your shelf, but you still can't get shelf space', said Wallace. 'You have to come together with so much and even then you wouldn't get shelf space. You have to buy your shelf space, there is no bargaining power [as a small manufacturer].'

Wallace's experience is by no means unusual. Small manu-facturers of chocolate and other goods have similar stories to tell about the difficulty they face in securing shelf space. Just as a handful of makers dominate the chocolate business, a small number of retailers straddle the high street. In North America, Western Europe and Japan, supermarkets' share of food retail-ing is estimated to be in the range of 75–85 per cent.[19] This concentration works against small companies. Larger producers have more muscle in an environment where shelf slots for new bars are fiercely contested. No one, for example, will refuse a new bar from a large chocolate company, if refusing it means they will withhold other popular bars.

In this context, negotiations with retailers are often detailed and complex. A large store may want to see a deal with a favoured distributor before they agree to take the product. Distributor charges and demands vary. In some cases, as much as one-quarter of the retail price goes to the distributor. One small American chocolate company told me that for every 50 cent bar a retailer buys from a niche producer, the food distributor takes 12 cents for delivery within the USA, just 4 cents less than it takes to make and wrap the bar. Retailers may make other demands. For example, in some cases the manufacturer has to pay for the storage of the product in the shop's warehouse. For a small company, this is a huge ask.

Once you are on the shelf, it is also easy to lose the slot. Most people buy chocolate on impulse. It is a split-second decision. They gravitate towards a bar they know or recognise, or even just the one in front of their face. Often the chocolate they will see is that made by Mars, Hershey and Cadbury, which has been backed up by an advertising campaign. 'There is a lot of investment required to get consumer attention', said Joe Whinney, managing director of Theo Chocolate, an American company. 'If you don't perform well, they kick you out quickly; it is easier to get on the shelf than it is stay there.' It is a confused and crowded market. Wallace's chocolate is actually made in Ghana. Many others, such as Divine, the Fairtrade chocolate company, source their beans from Ghana but do not make their products there. Consumers, Wallace fumes, often don't recognise the difference. 'Just to take beans offshore and package them is not a huge accomplishment', said Wallace. On a counter brimming with bars, it is difficult to stand out.

Nearly two decades later, the irony for a man who set up his business so he could spend more time in Ghana is that he spends most of his time in the USA, on the phone to retailers and distributors. 'Most of my challenges are distribution. Getting shelf space, holding on to shelf space, keeping shelf space, managing large retailers', he said. The upbeat and earnest Wallace retains his sense of humour about the difficulties of doing business. 'When I started, my big worry was someone would beat me to it. Maybe I have other worries now; it is not that worry', he joked.

Several things work against Wallace. There is no market within West Africa for his chocolate. He struggles to get the ingredients he needs. The dedication of customs officers and food safety officials in the USA make it, he jokes, the 'most inspected chocolate in the world'. His final battle is to get the finished products onto a supermarket shelf chock-full with sweets made by larger competitors. Wallace declines to offer figures, but says sales are rising, both in the USA and in Japan. He continues to secure deals with larger retailers and larger distributors.

But Wallace remains as enthusiastic and passionate about Ghana and his business as ever. If he hadn't owned the company, if he had been working for Nestlé or Cadbury's, then he 'would have been fired years ago', he said. Only a madman would do it, he laughs. 'I had a very supportive wife, who believed in me more than the project', he said. A sane man would have had an exit strategy by year five, he said. 'But it was my passion.' He tells me: 'I think our day will come, I am quite confident in that, the people that know recognise what we have accomplished … Any business endeavour worth doing is difficult.' Nearly twenty years after Wallace first set up the company, the country's expertise still lies with the cocoa beans, not with the chocolate bar. It is hard to see how that is going to change soon.

SIX

FAIRTRADE MYTHS AND REALITY

More to this than meets the eye

British pop singer Chris Martin is better known for his ballads and marriage to Hollywood actress Gwyneth Paltrow than he is for his love of Ghanaian chocolate. But in 2005 the Coldplay singer headed to Ghana with Oxfam to meet Kuapa Kokoo farmers. They grow the cocoa used in Divine Chocolate and own a share of the company, one of the UK's best-known Fairtrade brands. Farmers who sell their produce under the Fairtrade system get paid more and in Aponoapono, a Ghanaian village, growers told the musician what Fairtrade meant to them: a well with clean water, scales that weigh the crops fairly and better local schools. 'Fair Trade chocolate tastes better', said Martin later. 'But also it was amazing to go to a rich, green area like this and know that for every bar of Divine Chocolate you're eating, you're helping out the people who grew it for you far more than if you eat Nestlé.'[1]

The pop singer is not the only famous person to sing the praises of Divine and Kuapa Kokoo. The visitors' book at Kuapa's Kumasi headquarters is replete with well-known names. In 2002, Tony Blair visited a Fairtrade cocoa plantation in Ghana. A day before,

Harry Hill, the bespectacled British comedian, also paid a visit.[2] When delegates from the world's eight most powerful countries checked into their hotel rooms in Gleneagles, Scotland, for a 2005 summit which focused on aid to Africa, there was a complimentary bar of Divine Chocolate awaiting them, a gift from anti-poverty campaigners. These are the kind of endorsements most chocolate companies can only dream about: the prime minister of Britain, one of the country's best-known singer/songwriters, a popular alternative comedian and, to top it off, a seal of approval from the UK's leading charities. It is an unwieldy chorus of politicians, celebrities and anti-poverty campaigners. I was curious to find out why Fairtrade and Divine attracted such high-profile backers and wanted to know if the muddy reality on the ground matched the starry endorsements.

At first glance, it is not difficult to see why the great and the good throw their weight behind Kuapa Kokoo and Fairtrade. It appears to be a straightforward story of a battle for justice. In peak season, Ghanaian farmers spill their sweet, stinking dark brown beans onto a reed mat in a buying shed. Purchasing clerks name a weight and a price. The often illiterate farmers suspect the scales are fixed. 'They were cheating us', said Nana Kojo Appiah Kubi, one of the founders of the Kuapa Kokoo co-operative. Even after they handed over their cocoa to buyers, farmers had to wait months to be paid. Producers wanted a fair deal and scales they could trust. If they set up their own company, said Appiah Kubi, 'our farmers won't be cheated again'.[3]

Their chance came in 1993. Up until then there had been one buyer, the government. But a partial liberalisation of the market meant buyers could buy cocoa from the farmer at a minimum price fixed by the state. Purchasers then delivered it to the regulator, which exported it. Nana Kojo Appiah Kubi and six other producers set up their own buying company, the Good Cocoa

Farmers Company, or in Twi, the local language, Kuapa Kokoo. The first thing they did was to encourage farmers to check their cocoa on the scales against things of a known weight. Then the co-operative, with the help of Twin Trading, a British NGO, applied for Fairtrade accreditation. This meant their cocoa could be bought at a minimum price of $1,600 plus a premium per tonne of $150. To put that in historical perspective, in November 2000 the New York price reached a 27-year low of $714 per tonne.[4] That was a huge difference, and if the market price[5] exceeds the Fairtrade minimum, farmers would receive that plus the social premium.

But Kuapa's ambitions didn't stop at the farm gate. Backed by The Body Shop, the ethical cosmetic retailer, Christian Aid and Comic Relief, the British charities, farmers set up the Day Chocolate Company to make Divine Chocolate. By Christmas 1998, the first chocolate bars were on the supermarket shelves.[6] As consumers in the West bit into the rich and velvety Fairtrade chocolate, the Fairtrade money was used to build schools, hand-dug wells and water pumps, to pay for a doctor to travel to farmers in remote rural areas, and to make small loans to producers.

But the most important thing Kuapa offers, the one thing that no other buyer does, is ownership, Ohemeng Tinyase, then the managing director of the buying company, told me. Kuapa Kokoo is 100 per cent owned by the farmers; they take part in elections, choose their representatives on the board, attend annual meetings and decide how the money is spent. They also own a 45 per cent stake in the chocolate company. Tinyase, who grew up on a cocoa farm, is passionate about Kuapa Kokoo. 'I know how hard life is on a farm ... I see Kuapa Kokoo as the only company significantly impacting on the life of the farmer; nobody [else] is going that [extra] mile', he says, his voice rising. He added: 'There is no farmer who can say Kuapa Kokoo owes me or doesn't pay. Everybody in the cocoa industry, if the person is being candid and honest with himself, will tell you that Kuapa Kokoo is different from all the others.'

When I first arrived in Ghana, Kuapa Kokoo introduced me to farmers who said the kind of things Tinyase said. These producers talked about wells and schools, a lack of respect from other buyers and the importance of ownership. It seemed that what Chris Martin said was true. Farmers really were better off if you bought Fairtrade chocolate. Underneath the shiny wrapper, there was substance to the ethical initiative. But when I headed off to cocoa villages independently of Kuapa, the picture got muddier. Many producers didn't seem to realise that Kuapa Kokoo was different from other buyers. The ones that did sell their cocoa to Kuapa Kokoo also, they told me, sold beans to other companies as well. In fact, it seemed that whichever buyer arrived in the bush with cash fastest got their cocoa. To me, this didn't make sense. If Kuapa Kokoo paid a premium for their cocoa and invested in their communities, why would a farmer choose to sell his cocoa to someone else?

Other buyers, Kuapa's competitors, also raised their eyes to heaven when the co-operative was mentioned. The Ghanaian purchase figures, which are difficult to get hold of and rarely made public, indicated too that there was more to this story than met the eye. Kuapa Kokoo has seen its share of the cocoa market fall. In 1996/97, it bought 7,368 tonnes of cocoa, or 2.3 per cent of the crop.[7] By 2001/02, this had risen to 10.48 per cent or 35,568 tonnes. By 2007/08, it was still buying roughly the same tonnage – 35,052 tonnes, but its percentage of the market had fallen to 5.28 per cent. In the 2008/09 harvest, it bought 32,227 tonnes, a market share of 5.08 per cent. Farmers were growing more cocoa and production was rising, but many were choosing to sell their beans to buyers other than Kuapa. It was difficult to tally this fact and these figures with the glowing endorsements Kuapa and Fairtrade had received. Behind this story of farmer ownership and justice, celebrity backing and political visits lay a more complicated reality.

A global movement

The story of Fairtrade does not begin with Kuapa or Divine or even with cocoa. It begins with a coffee made from Mexican beans, called Max Havelaar. It was first sold in the Netherlands in 1988, at a time of crisis in the coffee industry. For decades producers had complied with the International Coffee Agreement, which set limits on how much individual countries could export. When this agreement collapsed, output soared thanks to new producers, such as Vietnam. But there was only so much coffee the world wanted to drink. The coffee price plunged and hundreds of thousands of farmers were on the breadline.

When Nico Roozens, a development worker with Solidaridad, a Dutch development agency, visited a coffee co-operative in Mexico in 1985, they were struggling to sell their annual output of 12,000 bags. For Roozens, their story echoed a particularly unpleasant part of Dutch colonial history, the ill-treatment of Indonesian coffee pickers. A novel written by a disillusioned Dutch colonial official in the nineteenth century, *Max Havelaar: Or the Coffee Auctions of the Dutch Trading Company*, had shone a light on the realities of colonial rule. For many in the Netherlands, Eduard Dekker, its author (writing under the pen name Multatuli), came to represent the national conscience, his book a story of the fight against oppression and unjust rule.

Mr Roozens wanted to pick up the Max Havelaar baton. He wanted to help Mexican producers sell their beans at a decent price. At first, his plan met with scepticism. Retailers doubted that consumers would pay a premium for coffee grown by a small co-operative. Roasters questioned if they could produce beans of a high enough quality. But Max Havelaar proved to be an unlikely success. Within three months of its launch, it accounted for between 2 and 3 per cent of the Dutch market for coffee.

The idea behind Max Havelaar soon swept through the charity sector in Europe and America. While Sara Lee and Nestlé, the goliaths of the coffee world, recorded substantial profits, farmers were poor. Activists hoped that initiatives such as Max Havelaar could change this. What in the Netherlands was known as Max Havelaar became known in the UK as Fairtrade and in America as Transfair. In the very early days, it was unclear what exactly these labels meant, other than that they indicated a desire to help producers. In 1997, the Fairtrade Labelling Organization was set up to hammer out some global definitions. A Fairtrade label meant that farmers received a decent price, one that covered the cost of sustainable production, and a bonus which they invested in their communities. To qualify as Fairtrade producers, smallholders had to be democratically organised – in practice this meant they had to join a co-operative – and meet minimum social, economic and environmental standards.

Kuapa was certified as a Fairtrade producer in 1995; with roughly 40,000[8] registered farmers, it is the largest such co-operative in the world. The hopes fostered by the success of Max Havelaar coffee and the Fairtrade movement were to collide with the gritty competitive realities of the Ghanaian cocoa market.

Not the only fair buyer

There is a slow build-up to the start of the cocoa season in Ghana. Farmers harvest the first ripe pods in late August and early September and leave the beans to dry on reed trays in the muddle of huts that make up farming villages. By mid-September, trees are heavy with yellow and purple pods. Speculation is simmering about the price for the coming season. Every year, the government sets a minimum price. Opposition newspapers suggest that this year the government will short-change farmers. Government papers claim that producers will get their due. Buyers make their rounds, but smallholders are reluctant to part with their beans. There is a chance the price will be higher than last year. It may be better to hold on to their beans for a week or ten days more in case they get a dollar extra a bag. By late September and early October, the speculation is close to boiling point. Then, with a snap of an official finger, the government announces the price and the season begins. The floodgates open.

This is the time of year farmer Joshua Nkrumah lives for. This is when he gets the money that will clear loans, pay for school fees, clothes and mobile phones. Mr Nkrumah may have just a couple of bags to sell but he has a choice of roughly twenty-five buyers. In the busiest cocoa villages, where there may be little other than a water pump and maybe a school under a tree, there can be as many as five or six buyers' depots, staffed by agents eager to buy their crop. These buyers have to pay the minimum price set by the government but many offer more: machetes, insecticide, school books, even loans. Mr Nkrumah, whose farm is near Hwidiem town in the Brong Ahafo region, has no loyalty to any one buying company. When I spoke to him, he said he may sell some beans to Kuapa Kokoo, the Fairtrade buyer, which pays cash, or to Produce Buying Company, the country's biggest buyer, which he says will sell him cheap insecticide but often pays by cheque. Several factors influence the farmer's choice of buyer. He may be indebted to one particular buyer and be obliged to give him his beans. He may choose to sell his cocoa to two or three buyers, spreading the risk that one may default on payment. His choice of buyer can also depend on who its agent is. He may be a relative or a friend. He may trust one more than another. The decision can be a personal as much as a financial one.

For most, cash is king. Many do not have bank accounts, and even if they did would not want to queue in a branch in a faraway town. When buyers come looking for cocoa, they want notes in their hand. With this in mind, purchasers need to have a lot of cash ready. During the 2010/11 season, farmers received 200 cedis ($140)[9] per 64 kilo bag.[10] There are sixteen bags in a tonne and Ghana produces an average 650,000 tonnes of cocoa a year. In any given year, buyers hand over roughly $1 billion in cash to farmers. It is not easy to get this kind of money. Usually they borrow it from the government, which raises finance on the international markets to fund cocoa purchases. Receiving this cash, known as the seed fund, is a slow process, prone to delays, and interest rates are high. Once the buyers have the money in their bank accounts, they need to get it to remote farms and villages. Banks in cocoa towns such as Enchi, Sefwi Wiawso or Koforidua don't necessarily have enough notes in their vaults. Some buyers count notes into the jute sacks used to transport cocoa beans and go to villages to purchase cocoa. Others charter vehicles, fill them with cash in Accra or Kumasi and head to farming areas. Those with cash at the ready will get their beans.

In this rush for cocoa, Fairtrade means little. For a start, Kuapa Kokoo, like other buyers, borrows money from the government to finance purchases and is subject to the same delays. It may have to wait for the money to land in its account or the bank to make cash available. From what smallholders told me, a farmer faced with two buyers, one of which is Fairtrade but without the ready cash, the other of which is not Fairtrade but with the money available, will likely choose the latter. A survey of more than 400 farmers by the Overseas Development Institute in 2007 found that the availability of cash was the 'key factor driving farmers' choices of whom to sell to; and the next most important reason for selling to a specific buyer is the availability of credit for inputs.'[11]

On top of that, the Fairtrade minimum price, though impressive on paper, means next to nothing in the bush. There are two main reasons for this. First, in recent years, the price of cocoa has risen, far above the Fairtrade floor of $1,600 a tonne (due to rise to $2,000 in 2011). Second, at the same time, the government has steadily increased the minimum price that farmers receive. For the past several years, farmers across the country have received a steady and rising price for their cocoa. This is true whether or not their beans are loaded into a Kuapa Kokoo truck or one belonging to another buyer, such as Akuafo Adamfo or Olam, because the price they receive is determined by the government. What this means is that farmers faced with a choice of buyers will not necessarily see that much difference between Kuapa and another purchaser. The government-fixed price frequently matches or exceeds the Fairtrade floor. For the 2010/11 farm year, all Ghanaian farmers received 3,200 cedis or $2,242 per tonne.[12]

Two factors could change this scenario and make Fairtrade a much more attractive buyer. If the world market price was to tumble dramatically or the government was to make a U-turn on its price policy, then Fairtrade could offer producers an advantage. But both, for now, appear unlikely. Farmers around the world are not producing enough cocoa to meet chocolate companies' demand. One analyst quoted in the *Financial Times* described these companies as living 'hand to mouth', desperate for cocoa beans, waiting for a price fall that seemed 'remote'.[13] As far ahead as most buyers and analysts can see, the price of cocoa is expected to remain high. But this is a cyclical crop. At some stage, prices will certainly fall again. 'It is fine while the market is high to say Fairtrade is not offering much. In 2000 the market price was $700; we were paying $1,600', said Divine's Sophi Tranchell. It is certainly true that the Fairtrade minimum price could protect producers from a future drop in price, but so too could diversification, the growth of crops other than cocoa, or improvements in productivity, which would enable them to harvest more cocoa from fewer trees. These latter alternatives are arguably more sustainable in the longer term than simply paying farmers more for their produce. The second possibility – that the government cuts prices – appears remote. If prices fall too low, cocoa could be smuggled to Togo or Côte d'Ivoire, thus depriving the Treasury of crucial revenues. This is a real risk and one the government is very aware of. More importantly, since the early 1990s, the country has had five democratic elections and two changes of power. There is no government that would take the votes of 720,000 cocoa farmers for granted. Government is under pressure to ensure producer income continues to rise.

The small size of the Fairtrade market also limits its benefits for farmers. Fairtrade farmers receive a social premium of $150 per tonne (due to rise to $200 in 2011). But demand for ethically branded beans is still low, and only those beans sold as Fairtrade will attract this premium. Until recently, Kuapa sold just 2,500 tonnes of Fairtrade beans a year, a small part of the roughly 35,000 tonnes it buys. From 2011, Cadbury expects to buy between 15,000 and 19,000 tonnes of Fairtrade cocoa a year. Assuming that Kuapa Kokoo receives a $200 premium per tonne for those 21,500 tonnes (Cadbury maximum purchases plus Kuapa's other Fairtrade sales), that means they will make $4.3 million from the Fairtrade premium a year. Split between the co-operative's 40,000 farmers, this equates to $107 per farmer or about $12 a bag (assuming sixteen bags per tonne). A farmer who produces three bags a year and sells them – at current prices – for $140 each will receive just under $36 more on top of the $420 he would have received anyway.

How does that stack up against other buyers? Many offer machetes, school books, insecticide or loans, some of which are competitive with the Fairtrade offer. If these local buyers – which transport beans from the farm to the port – are to make a profit, they need to ship as many beans as they can. This is a volume business, buyers told me time and again. They need producers to sell them their beans. They need producers to sell them their beans. This encourages them to offer farmers incentives, however small. One of the biggest competitors to Kuapa Kokoo told me that they advanced $400,000 worth of zero-interest loans to producers in any given year and were engaged in a three-year programme to train up to 10,000 farmers. Smallholders also received cutlasses and other equipment, with 300 motorised spraying machines – which cost $500 each – given away each year. This same buyer also ran eight model farms to highlight best practices for producers. Asked why his company did this, he said: 'You don't want farmers to start leaving cocoa and going to other crops. If they have higher yields, that helps them.... You want to work with the best set of suppliers.'

In practice, Kuapa does not deliver the Fairtrade premium as a bonus to individual farmers. This is because its members vote instead to invest the money in community projects, providing schools or water, training and loans through a credit union. These are indeed worthwhile projects. Kuapa Kokoo has also been keen to promote women within its ranks. I have certainly met farmers, teachers and pupils who are happy to be linked with Fairtrade and who believe in the co-operative. There are, the competing buyer said, a 'core set of farmers who get value out of Fairtrade'.

But Kuapa is not the only organisation to work with farmers or in rural areas. There are other organisations, initiatives and buyers that command smallholder loyalty and respect. Abrabopa, for example, organises producers into unions so they can borrow money to buy fertiliser. The industry-funded Sustainable Tree Crops Farmers trains farmers in how to improve their output. The Gates Foundation has pledged more than $20 million to work with cocoa producers in West Africa.[14] Cadbury is to spend $30 million over the next ten years in Ghana. Mars is funding research into the cocoa genome. The cocoa marketing board itself offers scholarships for farmers' children.

Kuapa's efforts are genuine and mostly well thought out. But, as the co-operative's Mr Tinyase admitted, not all farmers will understand or appreciate what it does for them. This is a crowded field. It can be hard for Kuapa to distinguish itself. Sophi Tranchell, Divine's managing director, admitted surprise at the number of competing buyers she had seen in small villages. But she said Kuapa had done well to hold its own against them. 'I meet lots of farmers who say they will only sell to them. Yes, I have met farmers who haven't joined Kuapa, so there are obviously other places to sell it to, and reasons why you might have a loyalty to something else, but I do think they have managed to hold their share of the market, over such a long period of time, in quite difficult trading circumstances', she observed. Kuapa is in this for the long haul, she said. By implication, other buyers or organisations could drop out if there is no market incentive to help producers.

And as the Fairtrade pennies mount, so do the costs. Not only does Kuapa finance elections for its members – a Fairtrade requirement – it also pays for regular audits by FLO, the Fairtrade certifying body. Kuapa's size means that audits take an average of three weeks, FLO officials said. These audits take place annually and cost between €15,000 and €20,000. FLO auditors frequently recommend that Kuapa be split into small co-operatives so that it can offer its members more effective services. Kuapa has said it needs to be the size it is so it can compete in the Ghanaian cocoa market.

It is little wonder that, for all of Kuapa's efforts, I met farmers who said they didn't see much difference between it and other buyers. Barefoot on his veranda, Nana Yaw Ofosu, the chief of Ojeibikrom, can barely see out of one cloudy eye. There are two buyers in his village, Kuapa Kokoo and Akuafo Adamfo. Kuapa Kokoo has provided a hand-dug well, Akuafo Adamfo has given free school exercise books. Says the chief: 'They are the same, there is no difference. They pay the same price.' Who he sells his cocoa to, he says, 'depends on who has cash'. He complained that the government has set a low price, but said that life for farmers in Ojeibikrom has got better, but not because of Fairtrade. 'It is better now with competition, we have choices, we look at where there is money, before there was only one place and you waited months for money', he says. The chief's words illustrate the reality of Fairtrade cocoa in Ghana. Kuapa is not the buyer of choice for farmers; it is not even the only fair buyer. It is one of many competing to buy beans.

A competitive marketplace

Kuapa Kokoo is only one part of Ghana's Fairtrade cocoa story. The Kuapa Kokoo farmers also own a 45 per cent stake in Divine Chocolate, a British chocolate company. The rest of the company is mostly owned by Twin Trading, a Fairtrade NGO. At first glance, it seems that this stake in Divine should deliver real benefits to farmers. Around the UK, workers and students have pressured schools, coffee shops and offices to sell Fairtrade products. Starbucks has switched to Fairtrade after complaints about its 'sweatshop coffee'. In London alone, the Fire Brigade, the Metropolitan Police, the Bank of England, the Royal Botanic Gardens, BBC Television Centre, Sadler's Wells Theatre and the Globe Theatre all offer Fairtrade products to their staff.

Fairtrade products are even on sale in the Houses of Parliament in Westminster. As momentum has increased, so have sales. Divine Chocolate sales rose by 20 per cent in the UK in 2007 on a turnover of £10.7 million. This is a fraction of the global confectionary market but it is an expanding business.

But Kuapa Kokoo's large membership means that, so far, the gains from Divine Chocolate sales have been very thinly spread. Farmers received their first dividend payment in 2007, a cheque for £47,309, a little over a pound each for its 40,000 farmers. Tinyase told me that the money would be used to help reduce its reliance on banks for funding. It was a small amount but a big first step, says Tranchell. 'If we get as big as we would like to get, the profit will be the most valuable part [for the farmer]', said Tranchell. Until it does get that big, Kuapa faces the same problem with the Divine dividend as it does with the Fairtrade premium. It is too small to make a material difference to farmers.

Divine faces tough competition, not just from industry giants but also from its ethical bedfellows. Consumers motivated by equitable considerations have a wide range of products to choose from. They can choose Fairtrade products or goods which have been certified by Rainforest Alliance or Utz Certified. They can now even choose products from Cadbury. In 2009, the chocolate group announced plans to purchase Fairtrade cocoa from Kuapa as part of a £30 million investment in the country. The taste of Cadbury is the taste of Ghanaian cocoa, and the chocolate group is motivated by a desire to secure its supply. 'Without sustainable farming', said Alison Ward of Cadbury, 'we don't have beans or chocolate'.

At first, I found it difficult to understand the role of the ethical initiative within the Cadbury programme. Asked why Cadbury decided to buy Fairtrade beans, Ward said: 'In a consumer market it is a really well understood label, the recognition is high ... people understand what it means, it is a really powerful ethical label for us.' This I understood. Prior to its Fairtrade announcement, I had received a clutch of emails from Cadbury's public relations department outlining its investment for Ghana. This had gained little or no press coverage. In sharp contrast, the group's decision to buy Fairtrade for Dairy Milk bars was picked up by newspapers around the world and was followed by a high-profile advertising campaign. Nobody understood or was interested in the fact that Cadbury was ready to spend £45 million around the world on cocoa producers over the next ten years to help secure its future bean supply. In contrast, Fairtrade secured it a lot of column inches, allowing it to take a public pat on the back for the millions of pounds' worth of work it was already doing in Ghana. Why choose Fairtrade, as opposed to, for example, the Rainforest Alliance, I asked. Fairtrade, she said, is a stronger brand.

Given that ethical consumers can now choose between Cadbury and Divine for their Fairtrade chocolate fix, how do the two bars stack up against each other? Neither is actually made in Ghana. A family business in Germany developed the Divine recipe and makes the bars. Making chocolate in Ghana would not be easy, it said, a fact to which Steve Wallace (see Chapter 5) can testify. 'If you were manufacturing chocolate there, you would probably need to import milk there. You then have to chill chocolate and bring chocolate back out chilled. Whether you could make a bar that would be desirable, popular and affordable using that seems quite unlikely', added Tranchell. 'Because you are moving all the stuff about so much, then there is the added cost of making it and having to chill it.' It is also difficult, she noted, to find a manufacturer in Ghana prepared to isolate Fairtrade beans from those destined for bigger manufacturers. There are certainly good reasons not to make the chocolate in Ghana. But the fact that the bar is made in Europe means that most of the value in the chocolate – the part where it is turned from beans to bar and then branded – remains outside of Ghana.

For a consumer concerned about child labour, it is not clear that buying chocolate made with Fairtrade beans, be it Cadbury or Divine, makes a difference. American charities often encourage people to buy Fairtrade chocolate because it is free of child labour. Global Exchange, one of the most prominent campaigners against child labour on cocoa farms, provides a link to Divine chocolate on its website and says that 'cocoa companies pay prices so low that many cocoa farmers cannot meet their families' basic needs. But with Fair Trade certified chocolate, forced and abusive child labour are prohibited.' Both the co-operative and the chocolate company say that the practice has been strongly condemned and farmers have attended workshops on child labour. But they also hesitate to say that there are no children on Kuapa farms. 'I think the word "guarantee" is a strange word; unless you are on every farm all the time it would be impossible to guarantee anything', said Sophi Tranchell. In a co-operative of 40,000 farmers, it is difficult, says Tinyase, to identify who is working for whom.

In early 2010, a BBC television programme found that some Fairtrade groups had been suspended for their use of child labour in Ghana. Fairtrade countered that this was evidence that its system of regular checks was working.

With child labour, just as with many other issues, there is a huge disparity between what consumers understand by Fairtrade and what the ethical initiative actually means. Cadbury's Alison Ward admits to a certain unease with the claims put out by lobbyists. 'We have seen people make all these claims for Fairtrade. It is about getting an understanding about what child labour is or isn't ... Are they migrant labour? Are they slaves? That level of understanding doesn't exist in a lot of the lobbying NGOs.

That is the challenge we have got', she said. Fairtrade does not make these claims for itself, but it is not in Cadbury's, Divine's or Fairtrade's interest genuinely to raise awareness about the complicated nature of child labour on African farms. That kind of debate could confuse the consumer message.

Cadbury has said it will absorb the extra costs associated with Fairtrade and will not increase the price of the bar. So if a consumer does pick up a Cadbury Dairy Milk, made with Fairtrade beans, it will cost him or her on average 25 pence less than a bar of Divine, which costs 80 pence for a 45 gram bar.[15] Neither Divine nor Cadbury offers a breakdown of their costs, so it is difficult to establish how much more the farmer gets, considering the shopper pays nearly 50 per cent more for a bar which is roughly the same size. In the guidelines provided in its educational pack for schoolchildren, Divine says that for every £1 chocolate bar, only 7 pence is used to buy cocoa ingredients, while 13 pence goes on non-cocoa ingredients. On that basis, the Fairtrade premium for cocoa should only count for a penny or two more on the price.

What accounts for the high price? Divine does contribute 2 per cent of its annual turnover to Kuapa. The company, a small-scale manufacturer, is clearly at a disadvantage to Cadbury, which benefits from economies of scale and manufacturing that Divine can only dream of. Most shoppers are aware that Fairtrade products cost more than their non-Fairtrade equivalents. In some cases it is clear that the extra money goes to the retailer. When Costa Coffee began to offer Fairtrade coffee, it charged customers an extra 10 pence per cup. Tim Harford, a journalist for the *Financial Times* who styles himself as the underground economist, calculated that the real additional cost was tiny – less than 1 penny. When he contacted Costa for an explanation, it decided to offer Fairtrade coffee on request, without the price premium. Costa, like many retailers of Fairtrade products, had taken a gamble that consumers would be happy to pay an extra 10 pence for an ethically branded beverage and increased the price.

When asked how its offer stacked up against Cadbury's, Divine pointed to its farmer ownership, regular dividend payments to smallholders and the share of the turnover it delivers to producers. 'Instead of buying from a company whose main legal obligation as a publicly listed company is to deliver profits for shareholders, consumers have the choice to buy excellent chocolate from a company that works closely with its farmer owners and represents a different way of doing business', Divine said. Kuapa's stake in Divine has also enabled the co-operative to borrow money at cheaper rates, it added. The chocolate company offers producers an actual stake in the profits of the chocolate bar, stressed Sophi Tranchell. 'That is empowerment', she said. 'We're doing something that's significantly different.'

But until such time as Divine's profits increase, the fact they own a stake in a small chocolate company will not mean that much for Kuapa Kokoo's farmers. How big can Divine get? Nico Roozens, the founding father of Fairtrade and creator of Max Havelaar coffee, estimates that roughly 5 per cent of people will pay extra for Fairtrade goods, but the rest of us will stick with our normal brand. He added: 'It is a niche with potential, but it is a niche.' The best way to view Fairtrade, he says, is as one of a 'rainbow of ethical initiatives'. Some of these initiatives will come from smaller companies such as Divine, others from larger companies such as Cadbury, whose motivation is to secure bean supply for future generations. Fairtrade is not the only answer to producers' problems, says Roozens. 'There are many people who think Fairtrade is a concept for the whole market. It is the only way to salvation', says Roozens. That, he says, is 'bloody nonsense'.

If Fairtrade chocolate remains a niche product, that means that Kuapa Kokoo's 40,000 farmers will own a 45 per cent stake in a small chocolate company, one which, though profitable and growing, is unlikely to match their expectations of ownership and wealth. Consumers make a split-second decision about which chocolate they will eat. Their decision may be influenced by price, taste or even celebrity endorsement. It seems clear that, whatever Chris Martin says, it will not make that big a difference to the farmer which bar of chocolate they pick up. Fairtrade focuses on one reality. In truth, there is a much bigger story to tell about the Ghanaian cocoa market.

Airbrushing reality

Carrying her 16-month-old son on her back and a basket of corn on her head, farmer Margaret Entwi looks an unlikely player in the global chocolate market. But in the previous year she sold nearly five bags of cocoa, or more than quarter of a tonne, the tiniest fraction of Ghana's average annual output of more than 650,000 tonnes. Those five bags helped her educate five of her six children, one of whom is at university. The sixth child is still on her back, whimpering and grabbing at cocoa pods, but his future is already bright in his mother's eyes. He will never be a cocoa farmer, she says. 'He will go to school and be a professor.'

Whatever chocolate you bite into, whether it is premium, luxury, organic, dark, or packed with nuts or fruit, Divine or Mars, it seems safe to say that the lives of cocoa farmers in Ghana have improved in recent years. Margaret Entwi's share of the market price has risen steadily from about 30 per cent in the early 1990s to the current level of between 50 and 60 per cent.[16] Thanks to that, and to a government spraying campaign to combat disease, production has increased from 340,000 tonnes in 2001/02 to a current average of 650,000 tonnes. The economics of the marketplace are in her favour, though prices remain volatile. Global demand for cocoa is steady, yet supply is weak. The fundamentals of the market support higher prices. Buyers compete for her beans and some offer her incentives on top of the state-fixed minimum price. Life in Ghana is improving. While schools may be overcrowded, primary education is free and compulsory. Producers' lives have clearly improved. But they have improved for reasons that have nothing to do with Fairtrade.

In fact, the real reasons for this improvement barely feature in the Fairtrade story at all. In the 1970s and early 1980s, the government underpaid farmers and production plunged. President Rawlings and his successor, President Kufuor, knew that without proper recompense for their produce farmers would simply stop growing the crop or smuggle it to Côte d'Ivoire, where prices were higher. So they increased the minimum price to encourage farmers to grow cocoa. Farmers are also now voters. In 1992, Ghana held its first democratic elections in two decades, after years of coups and military governments. There are roughly 720,000 farmers, and successive governments have recognised that the farming lobby is an important one. The price paid to farmers has continued to rise.

This reality is glossed over in the Fairtrade story. When Harriet Lamb of Fairtrade and Todd Stitzer of Cadbury went to Ghana, the Fairtrade press release read, they 'spoke to farmers about the modern-day difficulties of cocoa farming and discussed how increasing stability of cocoa earnings through stronger farmers' organisations and Fairtrade certification could deliver significant improvements to livelihoods, enabling farmers both to implement sustainable agricultural practices and to improve life in the wider community'. This statement does not withstand closer examination. Well-organised co-operatives or farmer groups can certainly make a big difference, making it easier for government and buyers to communicate with farmers and offer training and support.

But in Ghana, the role played by co-operatives and Fairtrade in improving farmers' lives has so far been limited. The government sets the price, and it is the government's decision to increase that price and to continue increasing it that has delivered income stability to the vast majority of the country's farmers, of which just 40,000 are Fairtrade.

Advocates of Fairtrade, such as Nico Roozens, say that the initiative has set the agenda for farmer welfare. But while Fairtrade might have set a marketing agenda, the agenda for sustainable farming and producer welfare has been set by market and democratic forces far greater than one simple ethical initiative. Companies are afraid they will run out of beans and want to support farmers to stick with the crop; governments want to secure future votes and revenues by improving the lot of smallholders.

Much more does need to be done to help producers. But the issues that need to be tackled now, those of diversification, land reform, rural banking and scientific research, lie beyond the remit of Fairtrade. Their resolution lies in the hands of the Ghanaian government and industry. Its advocates say Fairtrade offers farmers a voice in the world cocoa market. But the voice that counts is not that of Fairtrade, but that of the marketing board, which exports the cocoa on producers' behalf and has sufficient weight to secure a decent price for Ghanaian beans (Chapter 7). Far bigger factors than Fairtrade are shaping the country's cocoa industry.

The story told by Fairtrade airbrushes out the role played by governments, elections and world markets and homes in on one relationship only, that between the shopper and the farmer. According to this version of events, what matters most to Ghanaian farmers is which chocolate bar you buy. But Fairtrade did not bring about change in Ghanaian cocoa villages; Fairtrade has piggybacked on the democratic gains made by Ghana. The real change comes not from the split-second decision to pick up a bar of Divine but from the thumbprints on ballot papers, the counting of votes, the inauguration of new presidents, and the realisation that farmers are not just producers. They are also voters.

SEVEN

TRADING GAMES

Privileged childhood

For someone who grew up in the 1950s just a few hours from a cocoa farm, John Newman lived a life not dissimilar to an English middle-class child of his generation. His father was a civil servant and a lawyer and his mother a trader in Accra. He went to Mfantsipim secondary school, one of the finest in the country, and received an education, he said, that he would have been lucky to receive in the UK. 'I was taught how to play cricket … we learned the classics, I became a liberal scholar', he said. As he sped by in a school bus to cricket matches, he was struck by the sight of people walking on the road with goods on their heads. He was aware he had never experienced poverty himself and realised there were many who had far less than him. When later he studied law, he took a job first at the Ministry of Finance and then at the cocoa marketing board, which ran the country's cocoa industry.

Shortly after Newman joined the board in his twenties, he visited a plantation. This trip brought home to him what that line in the country's budget for cocoa revenues really meant.

Everywhere he turned he was greeted with images of a life lived in sharp contrast to his own. In the village, he 'saw the farmer drink bad water; I was offered bad water and I couldn't drink it. [I said] I will apologise, I can't drink it, the farmer said you *obroni* [white person] go away.' He was struck by his own 'extraordinary privilege' and how it contrasted with farmers' lives. 'This is the person who helps to create the wealth. I read economics; this is the microcosm of the wealth creator and I thought, look at me, I have never been part of wealth creation, I have gone to all the schools, I played cricket, I could have been lifted and dumped in the UK, and I would have been alright and yet I don't belong [there] I belong here', he said. He immediately linked these farmers' labour with his own privileged existence. 'The aggregate effort of all these farmers enabled me to have the kind of education I had; it is the cocoa farmer and timber operator who support the budget to enable government to fund education.'

The awareness of that link between farmers' lives and Newman's own upbringing has remained with him through a long career in the cocoa industry, which culminated in him heading the country's cocoa board. I met him at a cocoa factory in Tema shortly after I arrived in Ghana. At that time, he had left the Cocoa Board and was working as a consultant. He was passionate about cocoa and politics and genuinely eager to discuss the best way to improve farmers' lives. He articulated a sense of responsibility for producers that I found both unusual and sincere. No one else I had met in Ghana, Côte d'Ivoire or London seemed half as bothered as he did about producer welfare. Recalling his thoughts about the first farmer he met, he said: 'So this is the man or the woman who creates all this wealth and these are his conditions. I, if I should be in the industry, should do something which would enable him to move away from this poverty quagmire, this situation.'

Since that first visit to a farm forty years ago, the market in which Newman and the Cocoa Board operate has expanded far beyond what could have been imagined when he first started out. Global production has risen, trebling from 1.1 million tonnes in 1960/61 to an estimated 3.7 million tonnes in 2007/08.[1] The chocolate and cocoa-based products market is worth $75 billion.[2] In recent years, the large chocolate companies have become even bigger, while smaller ones have withered or been absorbed into conglomerates. At the same time, most farms resemble the small, scattered plantations that Newman saw on his first visit to the bush four decades ago. The Board for which Newman worked was set up to help farmers to get the best price possible for their produce. Its aim was to provide a link between the isolated village producer and the global trader. I wondered what role the Board could play in this new contracted world, where a small number of companies bought the world's beans. Could this Board work on behalf of farmers to help improve their lives and prospects?

Fundamental rules

How much is a tonne of beans worth? For someone who doesn't enjoy chocolate, they are worth very little indeed. For a chocolate lover or someone with a factory to run, they can be worth a great deal. It is virtually impossible to ascribe an absolute value to these beans or any other commodity. At any one time, hundreds of trades are taking place around the world, all of which help determine the present and future value of cocoa. Some take place in the capitals of Accra and Abidjan, others in the bush between middleman and farmers. Some of the most valuable trades are advance orders which take place in the global futures markets.

These advance orders are big business. Their value far exceeds that of the actual physical beans shipped around the world.

Billions of dollars' worth of deals are executed electronically by traders in London, Amsterdam and Chicago. These deals help determine the profits a chocolate company makes and the price a farmer receives.

If a trader anywhere wants to establish the price for beans, he or she needs to have a strong grasp of what is known as the market fundamentals, or the levels of supply and demand, how much cocoa is available for sale and how many people want to buy it. It is this balancing act between the heaps of drying beans in the village and the churning mills of chocolate factories that helps establish the price for beans. It helps determine how much money the farmer has in his pocket.

If a trader wants to assess demand for cocoa, he or she can look at the amount of chocolate being sold. As a general rule, sweet sales rise in line with world economic growth. If people have more disposable cash to spare, they are more likely to buy treats. Equally, traders can examine the grinding figures to assess demand. This data indicates how much cocoa is being processed into butter, powder and liquor, another sign of demand for chocolate and thus cocoa.

Traders who want to ascertain supply analyse news and weather reports from Ghana and Côte d'Ivoire. They are eager to find out what is happening on the ground. Rainfall in Kumasi, disease in Sefwi Wiawso or no sunshine in Abengourou can all inform their trading decisions. Crop forecasters, known as pod counters, travel to the bush regularly to assess what output is likely to be. They count the green oval shells which cling to branches. They look for the tiny white flowers or cherelles which blossom into pods. Their analysis surfaces later in internal company reports, written to help traders make the best decisions they can. These reports can be hugely influential. It is not unusual for the publication of a pod counters' report or rumours of their findings to move prices.

International cocoa companies and the Board dance around each other in this search for information about the crop. 'It is a very interesting relationship', said Kwame Pianim, former head of the Cocoa Board. 'You watch them, they watch you … but you make sure your big buyers are happy, you keep them sweet, so that they have good relationships with you.'

This need for information about supply is the main reason Reuters has a correspondent in Ghana. They wanted me to provide regular stories about output all year round. This kept me busier than you would imagine. International markets are hungry beasts, desperate for fresh information. News agencies such as Reuters are keen to feed them with stories the whole time. My bosses did not care if output was rising or falling. They had no agenda as such to push. They just wanted me to deliver a steady stream of stories. Their aim was to provide useful trading information to the commodity specialists who subscribed to their news service.

In order to write these stories about the crop, I headed up-country and spoke to farmers and middlemen. I spoke to the men who unloaded the bags at the depot and the people who checked the quality of the beans. I talked to anyone who could tell me if business was busy or slack. In Accra, I visited the Ghana Metereological Service to get data on rainfall and humidity. I interviewed striking transport workers, and a couple of times I counted the hundreds of trucks stacked up in Takoradi port so I could write about congestion and delays to deliveries.

On one level, this was highly mundane information, available to anyone willing to make the effort to get it. On another level, it was highly sensitive. A throwaway comment about shipments could move the price on international markets and affect Ghana's earnings. This fact made traders at the marketing board who sold cocoa on the international market incredibly nervous. 'When you have 60 to 70 per cent of the foreign exchange proceeds of your country coming out of your work, that is pressure', one of the Board's former traders told me.

Fear of moving prices made officials at the marketing board reluctant to say how much cocoa had arrived at the port, how many shipments had been made, and even if the weather was favourable for production. They didn't want to give me any information which would make it harder for them to secure an advantageous sale. Their sensitivity became clear to me soon after I arrived in Ghana. On my first trip to Kumasi, a secretary in the regional office of the marketing board arched her eyebrows and asked me if it was 'in the best interests of Ghana' for her boss, a senior cocoa official, to speak with me. When she allowed me through, he ducked my questions. It was more than his job was worth to tell me if the blue sky above us was good news for the cocoa crop or not, or if the rain of the past week would foster disease. The last thing he wanted was to be responsible for moving the price of cocoa on the world market.

Other factors also deterred officials from speaking to journalists, factors which made me question how the Board was run and if it really acted in farmers' interests. Stories on Reuters were often picked up by the local press. A forecast of a drop in output could be picked up by an opposition politician as a sign that the economy was being mismanaged. The simple fact that an official had spoken to Reuters could be used against him by a colleague or politician in what was a highly political business. Some wondered what my agenda really was. Was I using this information for my own financial gain? Was I really simply a journalist writing stories for an agency? Or was I working for someone else with designs on Ghanaian cocoa?

At first, I felt I could understand their reluctance to speak with me. Ghanaian traders wanted to get a good deal for their cocoa.

The stories I wrote could in theory send prices lower or give a buyer an advantage in negotiations. Their suspicion and wariness seemed understandable. But the longer I worked in Ghana, the more impatient I became. I felt that they used their fear of moving markets as a smokescreen. They were loath to talk to reporters about the crop, but it was commonplace for international traders to pay junior officials for any data they could get about cocoa purchases or shipments. I felt they were more concerned about hiding what was going on at the regulator than securing a good deal for Ghana. This lack of transparency bred secrets, misinformation and gossip. Few people in Ghana really knew or understood what happened at this organisation which bought and sold the country's cocoa on their behalf. I found it hard to believe that this was really in the country's best interest.

At the same time, the regulator responded pettily to perceived criticism. When I wrote a story for Reuters detailing the new farmer price in advance of the season, the Board responded by lowering it when the season opened. Two buyers later told me that the Board had changed it because it wanted to prove the news agency wrong. For an organisation used to secrecy and dictating its own terms, it seemed more important to teach a pestering journalist a lesson than to pay farmers the arranged price. One of my regular sources joked with me that I complained that smallholders were poor, but I had annoyed Cocobod so much that I had actually succeeded in making farmers poorer. In this environment, it seemed to me that more information about the supply of cocoa and the workings of the industry – not less – would have been a good thing.

The marketing board seemed more interested in covering its own back than it was in delivering the best deal for producers. I found it hard to marry the organisation I dealt with on a regular basis with the lofty aims articulated for it by John Newman. At the same time, farmers obviously needed some kind of organisation or leadership. I felt a well-run marketing board could be a useful tool. Not least because the groups buying their beans were drawing ever closer together.

A concentrated market

I was one of a handful of people who travelled to the bush regularly to assess supply. The others worked for large chocolate companies or processors. While they were few in number, they represented a huge weight of buying power. Mars Bars, Snickers, Kit Kats, Creme Eggs, Crunchies and Ritter Sport bars – the impression of competition given by the profusion of bars on shop shelves is an illusion. In 2005, Cadbury, Kraft, Ferrero, Nestlé and Masterfoods between them had 57 per cent of the European chocolate market.[3] In some countries, even fewer companies dominate the market. In the mid-1990s, Cadbury, Mars and Nestlé accounted for approximately 75 to 80 per cent of the UK chocolate confectionery market.[4]

There are a multitude of brands but a small handful of companies. Swiss food giant Nestlé owns Rowntree, the maker of After Eight, while Kraft, the maker of Oreo cookies and processed cheese, owns chocolate maker Terry's. Even the organic chocolate company Green & Black's is no longer independent. It is owned by Cadbury. At the time of writing, Kraft and Cadbury had agreed to merge in a transaction which would create the world's biggest chocolate maker. Once you strip away the silver wrapping and look behind the advertisements, there is very little real diversity on the shelves.

At the same time, industry boundaries have also become increasingly blurred. The main trading companies are also cocoa processors, which increasingly make industrial chocolate or couverture for large chocolate companies. The processing business is dominated by Cargill, Barry Callebaut and ADM, which between them control 41 per cent of global processing.[5] Petra Foods, based in Indonesia, and Blommer are also rapidly gaining in strength. The retail business is equally concentrated. In the UK Tesco, Asda/Wal-Mart, Sainsbury's and Morrisons have 74 per cent of the multiple grocery market. Supermarkets sell approximately 55 per cent of all chocolate confectionery retailed in Great Britain.[6]

The same faces from the same few companies turn up in Accra regularly to talk to the Cocoa marketing board about beans. In Côte d'Ivoire, local buyers or exporters often receive financing from these companies or are formally related to them. After a spate of mergers, the number of buyers has fallen, noted UNCTAD in a 2008 study on the sector. 'It is evident that allowing such a consolidation process has the potential effect of significantly reducing the number of real competitors in cocoa purchasing', it said. This puts buyers in a strong commercial position to buy beans at favourable prices and, despite current record levels, it is clear that this greater concentration in both retail and manufacturing has coincided with the long-term downward trend in commodity values. Figures from the United Nations' Food and Agriculture Organization show that, in real terms, prices in 2000–2005 were a quarter of what they were in the 1970s. In 2007, prices were still, in real terms, less than a third what they were thirty years earlier.[7]

Prices have also remained volatile. This is frequently blamed on speculative trade on world futures markets. Unlike commercial traders, who want beans for their factories, speculators have no interest in the beans they buy; they are simply making a bet. In recent years, many funds have put money into commodities, spurred on by reports suggesting a negative correlation between stock markets and commodity market performance. This theory suggests that when equity prices plunge, the price of sugar, coffee, corn and cocoa rise and vice versa.[8]

It is hard to assess how much money in the cocoa market is from industry and how much is from speculators. Funds generally downplay their influence on the market. Officials at the International Cocoa Organization said they had found no evidence that speculative activity had distorted prices. Anecdotal evidence varies. One analyst told me simply that a 'wall of money' has rolled into the commodities market in recent years. Whatever the size of their investments, an increase in speculative funds has made the cocoa market a noisier place to be, another told me. Prices can move suddenly and for no apparent reason, she said. These sudden price changes can have a big impact on farmers' income. It can make the difference between having enough to eat and struggling to get by, between keeping children at home or sending them to school. Producers are vulnerable to decisions made by people who have no interest in or need for the beans they harvest. For smallholders, the cocoa market can seem little more than a plaything in the hands of a few large companies and speculators.

Power games

This vulnerability of Ghana and Côte d'Ivoire to price movements on the world market surprised me. They were the world's two biggest producers. Why couldn't they exert more control over the market? I knew little about the oil market, but understood that OPEC's decisions on supply could move the price of oil in producers' favour. The oil producers' cartel met regularly and decided if and when to tweak supply. Its members spanned the globe, including countries as scattered as Nigeria, Venezuela, Iran,

Qatar and Angola. In spite of their geographical and economic diversity, this group could make decisions that moved the price of oil in their favour.

It seemed logical that the governments of Ghana and Côte d'Ivoire should be able to agree a deal on supply. Roughly two-thirds of the world's cocoa comes from West Africa. Outside of the region, the biggest producer is Indonesia. Between them, they should be able to play the game just as well as OPEC, which accounts for just one-third of world oil supply. The fact that so many beans were shipped from the Gulf of Guinea alone should strengthen their hand. In theory, Ghana and Côte d'Ivoire should hold all the cards.

When I looked through the history books, I found they had tried before. In the 1970s, producers agreed to hold a buffer stock of up to 250,000 tonnes, funded by levies, and set export quotas. By 1989, the fund was in arrears by nearly $90 million, with more than half owed by Côte d'Ivoire. The fund needed to sell cocoa simply to meet the annual maintenance costs. There were other problems. Côte d'Ivoire refused to sign up to the 1980 agreement, but joined the 1986 agreement, though the USA, the world's biggest consumer of cocoa, didn't.[9] 'Why they can't all band together', one World Bank official said when I asked him for his opinion, 'is because they see their interests as overwhelmingly different'.

This became clear in the late 1980s when prices tumbled on the international market. Côte d'Ivoire was struggling to pay its debts and President Houphouet Boigny blamed speculators for turbulent markets.[10] He decided to withhold cocoa from sale in an effort to boost prices. But there was already a surplus of beans on the market and buyers could afford to wait for Côte d'Ivoire to sell. At the same time, competing growers needed the cash and were happy to continue selling their beans. Boigny eventually backed down. Prices continued their slide.

Producers 'are in the business of saying "I want to produce more than I did last year", regardless of the effect on price, regardless of what we keep telling them', one official at ICCO told me. Jan Vingerhoets, the organisation's chief, added: 'The countries have never reached a political agreement [to control supply]. Every country wants to expand its production. Every country wants to expand market share. They are competitors.' Even if six producers, say Côte d'Ivoire, Ghana, Nigeria, Indonesia, Cameroon and Ecuador, agreed to control output by means of, for example, a common export tax, it is 'technically still extremely difficult to do', he said.

While oil suppliers can control the flow of fuel by the push of a button in a refinery, controlling the actions of the hundreds of thousands of cocoa farmers who produce cocoa is tricky. 'It is a tree crop. With oil, you turn the tap. You open it or close it. It is not that simple with a tree crop. Once you have planted the tree, then production is coming. It is not as easy as with oil', he said. It is simpler, he noted, for rich countries with small populations, such as Saudi Arabia, to reduce supply of a crucial export. It is a much more complex equation for poorer ones, whose populations are heavily reliant on cocoa earnings. Smallholders who want to earn money will plant more cocoa. And once they have harvested the beans, they cannot afford to wait for cash. They have debts to clear, mouths to feed and school fees to pay. This is a perishable product which can quickly turn mouldy in West Africa's humid climate. Holding onto cocoa simply means carrying extra warehousing costs, said Kwame Pianim, a former chief of the Board. 'If the price is low, and volume is going to be big, you are stupid as a commodity seller to hold the stock because you are just moving the warehousing from the buyer to yourself, because they know you can't eat it. Sooner or later you have to come to the market', he said. Another analyst said: 'Potentially, you could hold the cocoa market to ransom in the same way OPEC did in the 1970s, but it doesn't work.... The problem is the individual thinks – do you think I am going to sit here and not earn money? No, it is basically smuggled and it gets shipped.'

Cocoa-producing countries are a long way from exercising anywhere near as much power as OPEC. The big cocoa sellers have yet to show any real intention of wanting to do so. At the same time, chocolate companies and cocoa processors have consolidated their buying might through a series of mergers and acquisitions. And in the past ten years, as buyers have become stronger, producer power, already fragmented, has splintered further.

Battle for control

There was one other reason why officials at the cocoa marketing board were reluctant to speak to me. When I arrived in Ghana in 2005, they were still nursing their wounds after a bruising fight to retain control of exports. The marketing board was set up to provide producers with a stronger negotiating hand. It dealt with buyers on behalf of farmers, selling their cocoa in advance, a practice which enables them to pay farmers a fixed price. Similar bodies exist elsewhere. The Canadian Wheat Board, for example, is controlled by farmers, and is the largest wheat and barley marketer in the world. These boards have their critics but many applaud their ability to pay farmers a steady price. But Ghana has faced a battle to maintain control of its Board.

When Ghana first began talks with the IMF and the World Bank about reforms in the 1980s, the Bretton Woods institutions queried how it ran the cocoa industry. Cocoa had been the bedrock of the economy, yet farmers were destitute. For decades, the Board had overtaxed smallholders. Producers received just a fraction of the world cocoa price. At its peak, the regulator, by its own estimate, employed 100,000 people, roughly one person for every eight farmers. For the IMF and the World Bank, it seemed clear that if the Board was abolished and farmers dealt directly with buyers, they would receive a better deal.

But this push for reform angered the Ghanaians. Cocoa, said P.V. Obeng, a senior adviser to then president Jerry Rawlings, was 'the only chicken that was laying the golden egg; until such time as we can diversify, get other crops, we will not release cocoa into foreign hands.' Board officials were furious. 'What we thought was that the Bank and the Fund wanted to fashion us into a free-market system through and through without any recourse to the situation on the ground', John Newman, then employed by the Board, said.

> We believed that we had marketed our produce, we had maximised our earnings, we did not appreciate it that somebody wanted to change a system that was working to the benefit of our country. The idea of the free-market concept was not an issue. There is the Canadian Wheat Board. In Australia, there were monopolies. Why us? Is it because we were so small and so broke and we needed support of the Fund, this should be a conditionality, they wanted to change the way we operated our cocoa industry, which was the most important industry for us.

Newman also had several practical concerns. The Board employed people to check the quality of Ghana's beans, for which it earned a premium. Quality could drop if the Board was abolished and its checkers sacked, thus endangering this advantage. Ghanaian companies lacked the technical expertise and the access to ready cheap finance that their foreign competitors had. Large multinationals could squash small local companies. 'I was concerned about who was coming to buy the cocoa, because I knew that Ghanaian companies did not have the wherewithal to hold their own against big players. To begin with they did not have the technical know-how', he said. 'The Cargills and the ADMs and the Nestlés, they are huge players; all these small players would have gone. How could these small, almost minuscule, companies hold their own against these big players? It was a big concern for me.'

The Ghanaian administration was united in its defiance of this particular demand of the multilateral institutions. 'Sometimes they drive wedges in governments, isolate those who say no to their prescription [until] they eventually capitulate', said Mr Obeng. His negotiating team knew the multilateral institutions wanted a story of success to advertise the wisdom of their prescriptions. They knew that Ghana, which held its first democratic election in 1992 and was eager to sign up to other economic reforms, fitted that description and they understood how to play that fact to their advantage. 'Our stubbornness at that time and the search for a success story by the World Bank and the IMF in an environment where we were doing some things right compelled them somehow to back out of the fight', he added. At the same time, fearing it would lose control of the Board if it didn't reward farmers, Ghana started to increase the price it paid smallholders. The government's obstinacy paid dividends. Ghana introduced a partial liberalisation, where buyers purchased beans from the farmer and sold them to the Board. But it retained control of exports.

Côte d'Ivoire faced similar pressure to reform its cocoa marketing system, but unlike Ghana it had a weak negotiating hand. It was heavily in debt and needed help from the same institutions that wanted it to overhaul the Caisse de Stabilisation, a price stabilisation fund known as the Caistab. It operated slightly differently to the Board in Ghana but still paid producers a fixed price. While the Ghanaian Board had overtaxed the farmer, bank officials felt that at least farmers benefited from its commitment to quality. By contrast, outsiders struggled to see any advantage to the Ivorian system. The Caistab sold forward 'on a very opaque basis', a World Bank official who pushed for reform told me. Bureaucrats in Abidjan were living off profit from the beans, while farmers struggled. 'So many Ivorians were making money from various aspects of the rent generation system, the resistance [to reform] was ferocious', he added. But the government needed debt relief. Reluctantly, Côte d'Ivoire agreed to overhaul the system. In 1999, the Caistab was abolished; farmers no longer received a minimum price and instead negotiated with buyers.

The push for reform led to the creation of two very different systems for the same commodity, running side by side in neighbouring countries and producers. Which has delivered the better benefits for smallholders? Unpicking the impact of these reforms is made difficult by the different and evolving political situations in the two countries.

Ghana, which reformed internal buying but retained control of exports, now aims to pays its farmers 70 per cent of the money it receives for its cocoa, minus spending by the Board on mass spraying, disease control, fertiliser and scholarships. Without knowing its exact expenditure on these activities, it is difficult to assess how often it reaches this target. What is clear is that the producer price rises annually, with farmers receiving more now than they have done previously. Accra still operates, by and large, the same system it did when it paid farmers just 34 per cent of the world price in the early 1990s. Between 2003 and 2008, farmers received between 41 per cent and 66 per cent of the world market price.[11] An internal liberalisation has allowed local buyers to purchase beans from the farmer and sell them to the Board. But the Board still controls the export and shipment of beans. The structure of the Ghanaian system remains fundamentally the same, yet government returns more to producers.

There are a few different reasons as to why this is. Officials I spoke to were anxious to ward off further demands for reform from the Bretton Woods institutions. The easiest way to do this was to continue to raise the producer price. 'Ghana advocated and put in place reforms to raise the producer share of FOB [the free on board price]. They understood they had to do this', one World Bank official told me. At the same time, cocoa is priced in dollars and the devaluation of the cedi made it easier for the government to increase the farmer price without necessarily reducing its own tax take. Most importantly, since 1992, there have been five democratic elections and two changes of power. The New Patriotic Party and the National Democratic Congress, the countries' two biggest political parties, have their natural constituencies but have to fight hard to secure a majority vote. In late 2007, one year before the end-of-2008 election, several buyers told me that the Board would have to increase the producer price for the 2007/08 season. It could not go into an election year without being seen to reward farmers. Unsurprisingly, the price paid to smallholders rose from 9.15 million to 9.5 million cedis a tonne. This was not a big increase, but no government wanted to be seen to ignore the demands of farmers. As an electoral strategy, this cannot be guaranteed to work. Successive rises in the farmer price did not secure the 2008 election for the New Patriotic Party. But only a foolhardy government would risk alienating the cocoa vote by continually underpaying farmers.

The Ghanaians clearly continue to profit from the fact the Board can sell its cocoa in advance and fix a minimum price for farmers. 'Generally there is a premium for the forward position, and the Ghanaians are generally able to take that premium by selling their produce a year forward', a senior London analyst observed. 'Even if the market price is flat for a year, the forward premium still exists.'

There are disadvantages. The regulator can be caught out if prices rise after it has agreed a sale price for its beans, notes ICCO's Jan Vingerhoets. In this scenario, the fixed price it offers smallholders can be much lower than that offered to Ivorian producers, who have not sold their beans in advance. Some years, Ivorian producers who sell their beans on the spot make more money than their Ghanaian counterparts. This explains periodic spurts in smuggling. But the marketing board is in a strong position to support its producers, Mr Vingerhoets said. 'The Cocoa Board gives very strong support to the farmer, by its spraying programme, subsidised fertiliser and improved technology.' This intensive support means the country has sustained its reputation for high-quality beans. While the regulator runs with far fewer staff than it did in its heyday, it still employs hundreds of people to check bean quality, once upcountry at buying stations and a second time at the port.

While progress has been made, Ghanaian farmers could clearly do a lot better. Smallholders who receive 60 per cent of the world market price are still paying a heavy tax on their turnover. The Ghanaian system lacks transparency. It is not clear how the farmers' share of the price is calculated and what services he is being charged for. The system remains open to abuse. 'The Ghanaian system can work as long as it is used wisely, as long as the Cocoa Board is not bloated, and as long as the fixed price is not being used primarily for taxation reasons', said ICCO's Jan Vingerhoets.

Across the border in Côte d'Ivoire, farmers negotiate the price directly with buyers. This can mean they get a higher spot price than their counterparts in Ghana. But with the abolition of the Caistab, the Ivorians set up five institutions to regulate the cocoa trade and support the farmer. These organisations taxed the farmer heavily, and offered little support. Between 2003 and 2008, farmers in Côte d'Ivoire received roughly 40 per cent of the world market price,[12] less than they had received under the old Caistab system.[13] In 2008, one World Bank economist estimated that smallholders received just 35 per cent of that price.[14] Since then, the producers' share of the price has risen, thanks to tax cuts. Ghanaian farmers smuggle cocoa to take advantage of this. Notwithstanding this fact, in the first decade of this century Ghanaian producers have frequently received more than their Ivorian counterparts.

One World Bank official from the time offers a typically blunt assessment of why farmers didn't get a better deal under the liberalisation of the Ivorian system. 'It should have been highly successful, if they hadn't screwed it up by creating all these institutions to steal', he said. Improving the lot of farmers was never really on the Ivorian agenda, one export official told me. 'When I was living through these things, it was a fight to have a new leader of cocoa, it was not a fight to have a new system', the official said. A genuine attempt to give producers negotiating power would have been too radical. 'There has never been the political will to give power to producers. In an agricultural country, that is like giving them political power.'

This heavy taxation in Côte d'Ivoire might not have been so onerous if the money had been invested in farmer support or if the price had been fixed. 'If you had more political stability in Côte d'Ivoire, the system would have worked better. A free-market system with good and adequate support would have worked', said Vingerhoets. As the situation currently stands, there is no one who thinks the Ivorian reform has worked. One respected cocoa analyst simply described it as a disaster.

When you travel between the two countries, the differences are stark. The cocoa marketing board is the only cocoa exporter in

Ghana. It is impossible to do anything related to cocoa in Ghana without the Board's approval. As one of the world's biggest sellers of beans, it is a truly respected counterparty for large chocolate companies and cocoa processors.

Across the border in Côte d'Ivoire, it is not clear who speaks for producers. ADM and Cargill are among the biggest exporters of the crop. In theory, large companies are prohibited from buying beans directly from producer. In practice, many have warehouses upcountry. There is a multitude of ministers, co-operatives, companies and organisations that represent their own financial, ethnic or political interests. The heavy taxation of smallholders is a potent illustration of the lack of producer power, of the fact that in Côte d'Ivoire farmers don't have a voice that counts.

These individual political narratives make most sense when viewed on a larger canvas, that of the multi-billion-dollar global cocoa business. This larger picture offers the best vantage point from which to consider what farmer organisations can offer producers. There are few producer countries, but they represent millions of farmers, dealing with relatively few buyers. In most cases, smallholders have failed to organise themselves in any meaningful fashion. Ghana at least provides its producers with the stability of a fixed price. In Côte d'Ivoire, liberalisation has served to further entrench the buyers' power on the ground as producers' demands go unheard.

In a world where giant conglomerates are the norm, not the exception, it is hard to dispute that farmers should be better organised and have more effective representation. Advocates of marketing boards such as John Newman argue that these boards remain the most effective way to deliver benefits to producers. He remains adamant that the Ghanaian system delivers farmers the best returns. If 'our people who create the wealth can't even sell the produce themselves', then that means that 'we, as Ghanaians, could do something to help the farmer to earn more, by continuing to trade and sell forward and make sure the farmer is guaranteed a certain kind of price.'

But the effectiveness of this or any other producer organisation hinges on two things. Smallholders need to have a voice locally, one which can be heard by their own politicians. Second, the organisation needs to have a voice which can be heard on the world market. Unless that happens, the voices of the 2 million or so farmers in West Africa will remain little more than a whisper.

EIGHT

BUILDING A SUSTAINABLE FUTURE

Cocoa under attack

A fat white caterpillar wriggles on a dead brown cocoa leaf in the outstretched hand of Kojo Efriyah, a Ghanaian farmer. Its small size belies the damage it can cause. The bug, which he calls *Akrokom* in the Twi language, burrows into cocoa trees, causing green leaves to wilt and pods, heavy with beans, to shrivel. This fidgeting grub could destroy Mr Efriyah's crop and leave him short of the cash he needs to support his family. If Mr Efriyah wants to make any money this year, he must keep these insects at bay and his farm free of disease.

He faces an uphill task. Uprooted from South America, cocoa is a delicate plant. It needs the right quantities of rain, sunshine and humidity to prosper. Even if those three factors are in its favour, it could still be ravaged by disease. Producers in West Africa battle with black pod, a fungal infection, and insects. On farms close to Mr Efriyah's, black pod's telltale dark splotches were evident on ripe yellow pods. In a matter of days and weeks, these marks can spread like inky stains, turning pods black and putrid. If rains are heavy and sunlight is scarce, it spreads faster, destroying the crop and the farmer's income.

And then there are tiny insects, known as cocoa mirids, that can lay waste to a plantation. They pierce branches, leaves and pods, ingest the sap and kill the unripe fruit. So devastating is their impact that Twi-speaking farmers call them *Sankonuabe*,[1] which roughly translates as 'time to go back to the planting of oil palm', implying that it would make more sense to grow any other crop than cocoa, prone to infection and easily destroyed.

The threat that pests and disease pose to the global chocolate industry is huge. The history of cocoa has been punctuated by devastating outbreaks. Swollen shoot, a virus spread by insects, wiped out the crop in eastern Ghana in the 1930s. Farmers in Surinam and Guyana abandoned cocoa in the late nineteenth and early twentieth centuries after an epidemic of witches'-broom, an affliction which liquefies the beans inside the pod.[2] Output in Costa Rica tumbled by more than two-thirds in the late 1970s as frosty pod rot ransacked farms.[3] The same infection has halved production in Peru.[4] Most dramatically, an outbreak of witches'-broom in Bahia in the late 1980s nearly wiped out the harvest in Brazil, then the world's second-biggest producer of cocoa. It has struggled to recover. In 2008/09, its total output was just 157,000 tonnes.[5]

Fear of disease deters Ghanaian farmers from growing organic cocoa, a potentially lucrative market. This is why most of the world's[6] organic beans are grown in the Caribbean and Asia. Hardly any are harvested in West Africa, where disease is rampant. Around the world, in any given year, an estimated 30 per cent[7] to 40 per cent of all cocoa production will be lost to pests and diseases.

A serious outbreak could change the chocolate industry overnight. There simply would not be enough cocoa in the world to keep chocolate factories ticking over, to produce bars at the cheap price we have become used to. There is no producer big enough to fill the gap in supply should the Ghanaian or the Ivorian harvest collapse. 'If what happened in South America was to happen in West Africa, we wouldn't have chocolate. It would be a luxury good', said Julie Flood, global director for commodities at Cabi, the commodities research group. Chocolate lovers would have to get used to paying £3 for every treat.

The blackening pods and shrivelling leaves are the most visible signs of the need for change on the cocoa farm. They are, however, far from the only problem that the industry faces. For the last century, millions of people have made their living from cocoa in West Africa. Output has risen as farmers have cut down forest and put fresh cuttings in the soil. When disease struck, when the soil became tired, these producers did not buy fertiliser or invest in insecticide; they simply moved on in search of fresh earth to till. Their restless movement contributed to the explosion of West African output and the spectacular rise in popularity of chocolate since the Second World War. Consumers can enjoy all the chocolate they want at a price they can afford precisely because of the ability and willingness of African farmers to grow all the cocoa the world's chocolate factories need.

The cocoa boom of the last century was made possible by the ready availability of land and labour, not advances in productivity or technology. The average farmer in Ghana yields between 350 and 400 kilograms per hectare.[8] Roughly one-third of farms yield 137.5 kg per hectare,[9] about one-tenth of what experts say they should aim for. In spite of shockingly low productivity, manufacturers have continued to get the beans they need. But this system is now under severe strain. If smallholders are to make a profit and chocolate lovers are to continue to eat what they want, then the business of cocoa farming needs to change.

Chocolate fears

For a long time, the high rate of disease and low rate of productivity on cocoa farms simply hasn't mattered that much. Under the current system, production has risen from 1.1 million tonnes in 1960/61 to an estimated 3.7 million tonnes in 2007/08.[10] 'Looking back it is possible to see that most of the growth that has been achieved has been a result of planting new areas with cocoa', Alan Cook from Cadbury told officials at a 2006 cocoa industry dinner. Smallholders may earn little from cocoa, but for decades they have seen it as their best opportunity to make any cash at all. If chocolate companies wanted more cocoa, farmers in West Africa simply grew more. If chocolate consumption continues to expand at the same rate at which it has over the past thirty years, smallholders will need to treble production again. 'If that rate of growth is to continue, we will need to be producing, and consuming, about 10 million tonnes of cocoa by the year 2040', Mr Cook added. No one knows where those extra beans are going to come from.

Alarm bells first rang for chocolate companies when production fell in Brazil in the 1980s. Where would they get beans if output in Ghana or Côte d'Ivoire plunged, officials asked. There are relatively few countries with the right amount of sun and rainfall for the crop. In countries such as Malaysia, where conditions suited the crop, upwardly mobile populations had other choices than tilling the land. If chocolate companies wanted to get the beans they needed, they had to concentrate their efforts in the Gulf of Guinea. One analyst said: 'There was no country ready to take over; they had to help Africa.'

These fears about future output have been exacerbated by stagnating production in Côte d'Ivoire, the world's biggest producer, and Indonesia, the third biggest. During the 2008/09 season,

Côte d'Ivoire's main crop, the biggest part of the annual crop, was the lowest for fourteen years.[11] In the same year, Indonesian production fell 10,000 tonnes to 475,000 tonnes. Globally, the 2008/09 season was the third consecutive season with a production deficit.[12]

Disease, poor use of fertiliser, lack of investment and high taxes all account for the sluggish Ivorian harvest. A study by that country's agricultural research body, the National Centre for Agronomic Research (CNRA), found that 46 per cent of the country's cocoa trees were more than twenty years old. Older trees yield less. At the same time, Ivorian smallholders are poorly rewarded. It is little surprise that its output is weakening.

This situation could be turned around. There have been cocoa busts before and they have been followed by cocoa booms. Low prices in the 1970s led to shortages and then record prices in the late 1970s. Prices plunged in the late 1980s and then recovered to current levels. High prices could spur smallholders to plant more trees and invest in their holdings. But future crop expansion will be very different from the booms of the last century. The strategies employed by producers up until now have outlived their usefulness. Producers can no longer simply continue to cut down forest trees and plant more cocoa. A closer look at the situation on the ground makes clear why.

Owning land and sharing cocoa

One of the things that struck me when I first visited plantations in Ghana was how many people had a link to a cocoa farm. If I stopped off at a buyers' depot to ask them what deliveries had been like, someone who worked there was sure to start talking about their own farm. People who ran businesses in the city would mention a family cocoa holding and how well or badly it was doing. Many of these people did little or no work on the plantation itself. In fact they all had other jobs and lives far from their cocoa plot. So when I went to the farm, the people I spoke with there – those who were cutting down pods and clearing the undergrowth – often didn't actually own the land. They simply tilled it. Frequently, they were migrant casual labourers or sharecroppers.

This system, known as *abusa* or *abunu*, has definite advantages in an industry as labour-intensive as cocoa. A lot of hands are needed to pluck pods, clear weeds and harvest beans. Under *abusa*, the caretaker and his family live on the farm or smallholding, take one-third or one-half of the crop for themselves and give the rest to the landowner, who may provide inputs and then spend his time on other farms or business interests. Over time, the sharecropper, who usually plants food crops as well, can earn enough to buy his own land to farm. Under *abunu*, the farm holding can be split between the caretaker and the landowner.[13]

It is not clear how many sharecroppers there are. A study, sponsored by Cadbury, noted a high reliance on caretaker farmers, with 46 per cent of farmers surveyed found to be migrants.[14] Some caretakers can be slack in their approach to the farm. 'The caretaker doesn't believe it belongs to him. He has other things to do, he is not seriously committed', said Yaw Adu Ampomah, the deputy chief executive of the cocoa marketing board. What is clear is that when the time comes to sell the harvest, the cash is split between several different people, some of whom rarely visit the farm. What this means is that even at times of high prices, individual farmers may have precious little to show for their labour.

What happens in the village of Betenase (Chapter 3) illustrates just how quickly the money earned during the cocoa season can evaporate. During the busiest few weeks of the year, farmers tell me that 500 bags leave the village and surrounding area. This can mean that $50,000 arrives in the village that week, a lot of money in a settlement of roughly 1,500 people. But very little of that stays there. The landowner, often absent, takes his share, investing in homes or businesses in Accra or Kumasi. The migrant farmer takes his cut, frequently sending the money to his home town. Others repay moneylenders. Cocoa money supports millions of people, not just those who work the farm but also many who have never harvested a pod.

The abundance of sharecroppers also served to highlight the confusion over land ownership. Several times, I followed farmers down slopes and through streams to the piece of earth they tilled. They knew the land intimately and could see boundaries where I saw nothing but a small clutch of trees. But I was not alone in my confusion. Disputes over land ownership are not unusual. While local chiefs are vested with authority to look after the land for future generations and cannot sell it, they may lease it. Problems can emerge once the land is rented. It may have been let to more than one person. Relatives of the chief may claim to have the right to farm or build on it. Fields left fallow or empty for any period can attract people eager to plant or start construction. Even though it is technically not possible to buy land, it is not unusual to meet producers who say they have done so. So far as they are concerned, the transaction that took place is final. But a caretaker's right to farm may be disputed when the original owner of the farm dies and a relative succeeds him. As land is passed through the generations, plot sizes get smaller.

These problems are not unique to rural areas. A friend of mine in Accra has a piece of land in Kokrobite, on the city's outskirts, where he hopes to build a home for his family. He doesn't have enough money to start yet but he visits the plot at least once a week. That way, he can be sure that no one else will start building there.

The Ghanaian and Ivorian countryside is a patchwork of small plantations, farmed by workers with complex and sometimes fraught relationships with the landowners.

But increasing the size of holdings will not in itself deliver greater efficiencies or profits. Attempts to grow cocoa in plantations in Malaysia highlight another reason why the crop is mostly grown by smallholders. 'You cannot say to a worker do the same thing for every cocoa tree. You can do it easily with oil palm. That suits large plantations. With cocoa, the farmer has to care about each tree, he has to see each tree as an individual', argues Jan Vingerhoets, of the International Cocoa Organization. Cocoa simply doesn't suit plantations, he said. An industry chief executive said: 'Doing everything in the same way actually didn't work [on cocoa plantations].' Cocoa is one of the few crops, if not the only one, in the world which is cheaper to grow on a smallholding than a plantation, he added.

Uncertainty over ownership can foster other problems. The absence of a title can make it difficult to borrow money at a reasonable rate, forcing farmers to rely on moneylenders. In Côte d'Ivoire, disputes over tenure have ended in bloodshed (see Chapter 2). The countless ways in which producers gained access to land helped foster the cocoa boom. But these complex relationships can also make it difficult for farmers to move out of poverty.

Need for science

Mr Efriyah's holding in the Ahafo Ano district in the Ashanti region is light years away from farms in the West. In West Africa, farmers learnt their trade from their fathers and grandfathers and till plantations barely a few acres in size. Their only tool is a machete, their only assistance is their family. Small, subsistence, hand-to-mouth, cocoa farming appeared to be everything that modern agriculture is not. In fact, it is misleading to describe these producers as farmers, said Howard-Yana Shapiro, chief cocoa scientist at Mars. Farming implies a level of expertise and business skill they don't have. They frequently lack the skills or knowledge to tackle disease. Too often, he said, they are simply gathering ripe pods.

Other experts recognise the haphazard approach to production outlined by the Mars scientist. Added Hope Sona Ebai of the Cocoa Producers' Alliance:

> I believe that not every cocoa farmer in West Africa should be in cocoa; some of them don't have the type of farm, in the type of state, to really call it a cocoa farm ... you have these trees that don't deserve to be alive, so we are not efficient. The farms are old, the farmers are old, the technologies are available in the research centres but that is it, it is not getting out to the farmers.

West African producers simply need to change their approach, he said. 'It is really nothing new. I think that we haven't approached cocoa as an agribusiness; when we start to do that, then the whole concept of cocoa farming will change.' Jan Vingerhoets at ICCO added: 'There are a number of farms that do not deserve the name cocoa farm ... There is some cocoa, maybe one or two hectares. It is neglected but some harvesting is done. That is not real cocoa farming.' One industry source in Abidjan said: 'This business model is not viable. We are sustaining, supporting, a business model that cannot deliver; it is absolutely nonsense.'

The problems faced by African farmers are steep. Disease is a perennial concern and agronomists question the health of the soil. Cocoa is rough on land, requiring fertiliser, which farmers can barely afford to buy. 'There is a lack of essential nutrients; they have mined the soil for the past hundred years. Imagine going to the bank and taking some money, and the next day and the next day, and you don't put any in', said Mars's Mr Shapiro. Farmers can return to exhausted and tired plantations and replant them with new high-yielding seeds. But this is so high-risk that it is akin to the lottery, another analyst said. For every three trees planted, only one may make it to maturity, he said. Fertiliser can help, but in parts of Côte d'Ivoire and Ghana they have grown cocoa for more than a century, which makes re-fertilising soils a long and expensive process.

West Africa's cocoa boom also came with a heavy environmental price. The forest clearance necessary to produce cocoa may have destroyed the nutrients in the soil that feed the cocoa trees. On plantations where few forest trees remain, 'there is much less biodiversity, the communities of wildlife are much less rich', said Professor Ken Norris of the University of Reading, who has led research teams in Ghana. The more forest trees that have been removed, the more difficult it can be to sustain the health of the soil. Efforts are underway to see if farmers can be paid to keep the remaining forest trees. This would not only improve soil health in the long term but would also boost their own earnings. This is a long-term project and is still in its early stages. The links between land, cocoa and the ecosystem need to be more fully explored if cocoa is to be sustainable, not just financially but also environmentally.

Until recently, cocoa hasn't benefited from as much scientific scrutiny as other crops. It is an orphan crop, ICCO's Vingerhoets said, explaining that it 'has never been part of the global network for agricultural research'. What this has meant in practice is a shocking lack of scientific knowledge on the ground.

There is a lot that can be done. Mr Shapiro is leading efforts to sequence the cocoa genome, to decode the million or so parts that make up the seed of a cacao tree. This should equip scientists with a tool box, one whose contents could lead to higher-yielding and sturdier trees, he said. The results of his research, part-funded by the US Department of Agriculture, will be made freely available.

The motivation for these efforts has never been clearer. 'We would like to be in the chocolate business in the next hundred years', said Mars's Mr Shapiro. 'We would like it to be there for [the next] three or four more generations of the Mars family.' This information is of little practical use if it stays in laboratories. Just as important to the future of the cocoa business is the need for farmer education and training.

On-the-ground training

Mr Efriyah points with his machete to a damaged tree and asks me what he should do. Many farmers, faced with disease, cut back the canopy of leaves overhead to allow the sun to penetrate and drive the bugs away, hack away the shrivelled pods and hope that others won't wither, or buy insecticide. But Mr Efriyah seems at a loss. His lack of knowledge is not unusual, nor is it confined to how best to tackle disease.

Considering the size and importance of West African cocoa output, it was a shock to find that when I asked farmers how many bags they expected to harvest or what their yield per acre was, their responses were incredibly vague. Many offered only a rough guess as to the size of their farms. If their farm was small, they would say between 5 and 10 acres; if they felt it was big, they would say it was between 20 and 30 acres in size. All figures were approximations, corresponding, I felt, to the farmer's sense of his own prosperity not to the actual size of the plantation. Farmers had a feel for the crop and a strong sense of what it was likely to be in the months ahead. They could interpret the weather and the condition of the trees. But I frequently felt they were unsure as to how much they had actually harvested in a given period and from a certain plot. There were difficulties in translation and communication. It took me a while to realise that they might be talking of the share of the crop they had received, not what they were about to harvest. But few seemed to keep records and it was rare that I met a farmer with a cash-book and details of his earnings.

Chocolate companies have funded initiatives to help fill this knowledge gap. The Sustainable Tree Crops Program (STCP) – a joint initiative of USAID and the chocolate industry – organises and funds farmer field schools. I attended one in eastern Côte d'Ivoire. There in a forest in the village of Oforiguie farmers discussed the cocoa trees that surrounded them. What do these brown speckles on a cocoa pod mean? Do these trees need to be cut back? What damage can these winged and crawling insects do? Some knew the answers or could guess them. Others looked to Lasme Celestine, the STCP-funded trainer, for his response.

Mr Celestine will meet these farmers once a fortnight over the next two cocoa seasons. During that time, farmers will learn the best way to manage trees, how to prune them and what distance apart to plant them. Farmers who understand what is happening on their plantation, how to diagnose diseases, prevent and treat them, will produce more cocoa without necessarily having to spend much money on insecticide and fertiliser. Attendance at these farmer schools can pay off. Trained farmers can see their yields rise by between 15 and 25 per cent, officials at STCP told me. Simply put, trained farmers produce more beans.

Courses like these clearly benefit farmers, but I did feel twinges of scepticism about plans to boost productivity. These initiatives are by and large industry-led. Officials I spoke to in the Ghanaian

Board seemed enamoured with the idea of increasing production, which would, in the short term at least, boost earnings. But I felt it was in the chocolate company's interests to push farmers to produce more beans. Many were rattled by the record rise in prices in 2008 and wanted to secure future deliveries. Could the push towards productivity just mean an endless supply of cheaper and cheaper beans, and even smaller earnings for smallholders? 'You can still provide cocoa at acceptable prices if you increase productivity', admitted ICCO's Vingerhoets. Was this really in farmers' interest?

I could also see that increased productivity could provide smallholders with more choices. If farmers trebled or quadrupled their yields, as experts believed was possible, they could grow the same amount of beans from fewer trees and use the spare land to grow other crops as well. Diversification could offer producers stability of income. Smallholders get 80 per cent of their cocoa from 20 per cent of their trees, said Shapiro. 'What does that [those trees] give to you if it only takes up space? Cut it down and put in something to feed your children', he said. The potential is huge. But risks remain. Government leadership is needed to ensure that smallholders do not just flood the market with beans but make the best of the opportunities presented by technology.

As things stand, there is a huge gap between this ideal of a trained, informed businessman and the reality of the pod gatherers described by Shapiro. Most smallholders receive little or no instruction in the business or science of cocoa farming. This is largely because Ghana and Côte d'Ivoire were forced to cut back their extension services as part of sector reforms in the 1990s. Courses such as the one run by Mr Celestine can help bridge that gap. Roughly 30,000 farmers have participated in similar training since 2003.[15] Another 65,000 or so have been taught by other producers. This is a tiny proportion of the 2 million farmers who live and work in West Africa. It is clearly in the industry's interests to provide this guidance. Increased productivity can help farmers make better use of their land and increase their income. It could give them more options at a time when Ghana and the nature of its economy are changing.

Lure of the city

The southernmost part of Ghana is a desolate spot. At the end of a long, long road, baby goats scurry and skid in the dirt next to mud-brick houses shaded by palm trees. Women leave fish to dry in front of their low-rise shacks. On a beach strewn with rubbish, children clamber over dozens of small fishing boats. Apart from the 'Lovers drinking bar', the St Theresa of Avila Catholic Church and a lighthouse on a hill, the village of Cape Three Points itself has little to offer. 'They have a sweet name but the town is not good', my driver observed.

But a few hundred kilometres west of here, deep beneath the sea, lies what could be Ghana's economic future. Ghana is to become Africa's newest oil producer, joining neighbouring Côte d'Ivoire, which has also recently started producing oil. The income from oil could change Ghana and Côte d'Ivoire. Oil revenues account for 6.5 per cent of total revenue in Côte d'Ivoire.[16] Ghana, when oil comes onstream in 2010/11,[17] is expected to earn $1 billion a year from the commodity.[18]

Both countries need only look to Nigeria to see what the discovery of oil could mean for cocoa. There, distracted by oil revenues, the government neglected the crop. Only in recent years has it started to try to revive the sector.[19]

Oil brings other dangers. In Nigeria, the oil-rich delta is home to battles between militants and Shell, the oil company working

in the region. Local people feel cheated by the large companies
that drill for oil and a government that squanders revenues. In
spite of the country's billions of barrels of reserves, ordinary
Nigerians remain poor.

Could this happen in Ghana and Côte d'Ivoire? Many are
sceptical about the discovery, the memory of the misuse of
cocoa funds still fresh in their memory. 'We have cocoa, we
have diamonds, we have gold. These three things haven't changed
Ghana. How can oil change Ghana [for the better]?' taxi driver
Nicholas Clottey asked me. Economist Nii Moi Thompson said:
'It could help us develop faster or it could create a whole new set
of problems.' Already questions have been asked about how the oil
contracts in Ghana were awarded.[20] The government has sought
advice on how best to utilise its oil revenues. In neighbouring
Abidjan, activists have called for greater transparency in the
Ivorian oil sector.

The discovery of oil also raises other concerns. When I returned to Accra after my visit to Cape Three Points and nearby
Axim, I was asked if I had met many job-seekers. The answer
was no. At that stage, in late 2009, there was actually little there
to attract people in search of work. Even when production starts,
there are likely to be few jobs available on oil rigs themselves. Oil
is a capital-intensive business that requires millions of dollars'
worth of equipment but relatively few workers. The question is,
however, pertinent. The oil money is likely to result in construction and labouring work onshore. Will people struggling to make
a living from cocoa really stick on the farm when riches beckon
further south?

It is not hard for Yaw Adu Ampomah, the deputy chief executive of the marketing board, to understand why someone
would want to leave his home village in search of opportunities
elsewhere, even if those opportunities are thin on the ground.

Cocoa is hard work for scant reward. By one estimate, cocoa households in Ghana are estimated to have a mean per capita daily income from the crop of US$0.42.[21] In cocoa villages, 'there is no electricity, no water, the roads are poor, the schools are not there, the health services are not there', he said. 'A young person looks at a farmer and asks himself, "Am I going to look like this?"' The average age of a cocoa farmer is 51.[22] The average Ghanaian life expectancy is 58. If the industry is to have a future, it needs to be attractive to an educated youth. 'An old person cannot use the land. He has not been to school, the documentation is poor, the youth can do it properly', said Mr Adu Ampomah. As things stand, it is not at all clear where the next generation of cocoa farmers will come from.

For this generation, city life presents a host of compelling opportunities. In late 2008, a new mall opened in Accra, the first of its kind in Ghana. When I visited on a Saturday afternoon, cars were jammed at the entrance. Inside, small children drove electric cars in a play area and teenagers hung out in fast-food joints. Their parents shopped for widescreen televisions, and browsed in stores selling Puma and Dior. There are bars, restaurants and the Silverbird Cinema, Accra's first. It was crammed full of people with money, eating popcorn and drinking Coca-Cola, visiting restaurants and shops.

This is a young, urban and mobile world, a few hours drive from the farm. Here 14-year-olds are teenagers, dressed in American clothes, not labourers on a farm, slicing pods from cocoa trees, hoping that October brings the right amount of sunshine and rain to secure a good harvest. In the city, you can earn a monthly income, however small. In the city, you don't have to wait for the main crop to start before you can make money. This is another world from the farm and it is not hard to see its attraction.

If life on the farm stands any chance of competing with life in the Accra Mall, then producers need to be able to make a decent living, observed Mr Adu Ampomah. Better yields can lead to an 'obvious improvement in their lifestyle'. Land reform is a thorny issue, one likely to be dealt with in the longer term, but other issues can be dealt with now, he said. 'The first part of it is to ensure that [yields] are up. The youth will be enticed.' The big city is attractive but rarely delivers on its promise, he said. Already, young people leave their villages to sell sundry items on street corners in the capital. 'If a youth selling dog chains in Accra gets back and sees farmers have done well, he may return.'

It is easy to forget that cocoa is a cash crop, so-called because it delivers cash to people's pockets. Yet cocoa, if it receives serious investment and is properly managed, has the potential to deliver real prosperity to people in rural areas. Already, there are a range of small-scale initiatives on the ground. The Gates Foundation and the Sustainable Tree Crops Program are all working to train farmers. Mars and other companies are carrying out scientific research. Cadbury is part-funding farmer extension services in Ghana, one slice of its £45 million ten-year investment in the sector across the world. To have real impact, these initiatives need to be scaled up and have the full weight of government backing, and producers need a government motivated to protect their interests. This is a serious issue not just for the future of the chocolate industry but also for millions of people in rural areas. There is real chance for prosperity here, one that should not be missed.

EPILOGUE

When I told people I was writing a book about cocoa, I frequently ended up being asked which was the best chocolate to buy. The people who asked me this question often distrusted large companies and wanted to buy chocolate from a company which looked after smallholders. They had read about child labour on plantations or maybe they already bought Fairtrade. As someone who knew about cocoa, which bar would I recommend? I struggled to find an answer.

Part of the reason was my natural scepticism as a reporter. I questioned if ethical brands really delivered the benefits they promised to producers. I felt that Fairtrade in Ghana was only one part of a complicated political and economic story. I didn't feel able to recommend one single brand, no matter how noble their intent or how worthy the cause. I felt farmers' problems were big and complex, and the more I got to know about the chocolate industry and West African politics the more I questioned if a consumer ethical initiative could resolve the difficulties faced by smallholders.

In some cases, I felt the questioners had been confused by simplistic or misleading campaigns. Reports on child labour often failed to mention that the Ivorian government levied heavy taxes or that there had been a war in Côte d'Ivoire. To me, these factors could be just as likely to influence smallholders' use of child labour as the price they received at the farm gate from an ethically branded buyer. Many reports exaggerated the incidence of child slavery. This didn't spur West African politicians into action. It simply raised hackles, cementing the perception that few in the West understood the nature of poverty or what life was really like on a plantation. At the same time, I have never read a report that mentions that the Ghanaian government pays producers a price that exceeds the Fairtrade minimum. Too often, the light shed on conditions in West Africa was skewed.

At the same time, it was unclear to me what ethical initiatives and certified cocoa really meant for smallholders on the ground. Were farmers being helped to become professional producers? Were they being taught how to rotate crops and encouraged to diversify? Did they have a business plan in place? Were they being paid extra for good quality? Or were they simply receiving an extra dollar a bag for signing up to the scheme? Too often, I felt that an ethical label and a higher price on the shelf was as likely to mean extra profit for the manufacturer or retailer as it was to mean greater rewards for the farmer.

There are certainly things chocolate companies can do to improve producers' lives. They need to commit to transparency in their dealings in West Africa. They should invest in scientific research, train farmers to become better at business and help them to improve their yields. Properly managed, these are all things which could improve smallholders' incomes. I also think it is in their interest to do this. Producers need to be able to make enough money from cocoa if they are to continue harvesting the beans. If not, a time will come when they simply plant another crop.

I also knew that in some cases farmers' lives had improved. In Ghana, smallholder prices are rising. This decision to increase producer prices cannot be laid at the door of one particular charismatic leader. Nor has it happened in response to an event or a particular consumer campaign. The initial trigger was pressure from institutions such as the IMF or the World Bank to reward smallholders. This pressure was sustained by regular polls. None of the main parties can be assured of their grip on power. They each have their natural constituencies and their detractors. Elections every four years mean they are eager to keep cocoa farmers on their side. A closely fought election in late 2008 underlined the fact that no one can take voters or farmers for granted. This can help push producers' share of the farm-gate price higher. Ghana could certainly do more. At the time of writing, farmers were receiving roughly half the international price. But it would be churlish not to recognise the progress that has been made. By the same token, I know that an effective dictatorship in Côte d'Ivoire has meant that producers' voices go unheard.

It seems clear that producers need a stronger voice at home and abroad. Effective leadership at home could ensure that producers do not flood the market with cheap beans, but instead boost their income by mixing high-yielding cocoa trees with other crops. Smallholders also need representatives to negotiate a decent price for their produce; they need a voice loud enough to be heard by the handful of multinationals that dominate the trade.

The merger between Kraft and Cadbury will mean one less buyer in a market already dominated by very few companies. This transaction could contribute to a situation where producers receive lower prices. Smallholders need to make a decent living if they are to continue growing these beans. At some stage, they may simply choose another crop or livelihood. This could mean chocolate lovers may no longer be able to get all the chocolate they want at a price they can afford.

Properly informed consumers could provide an impetus for action. But simply choosing one bar instead of another will not help resolve deep-rooted issues. Other forces, such as the balance of industry power and regular elections are just as important in bringing about change. By all means buy Fairtrade, Rainforest Alliance, Cadbury or Mars. But look behind the marketing. And don't forget to read the small print.

NOTES

INTRODUCTION

1. International Cocoa Organization (ICCO), *Quarterly Bulletin of Cocoa Statistics*, vol. 35, no. 4, Cocoa Year 2008/09.
2. Kwamina Dickson, *A Historical Geography of Ghana*, Cambridge University Press, Cambridge, 1971, p. 165.
3. Nowell Commission Report on the Marketing of West African Cocoa, Cmnd 5845, National Archives, Accra, Ghana, 1938, p. 15.
4. Report of the Commission on Economic Agriculture in the Gold Coast, 1889, National Archives, Accra, Ghana, p. 123.
5. Lowell J. Satre, *Chocolate on Trial: Slavery, Politics and the Ethics of Business*, Ohio University Press, Athens OH, 2005, pp. 112, 113.
6. Interview with Cadbury officials, Accra, October 2007.
7. Paul Davis, Federation of Cocoa Commerce dinner, 22 May 2009, London.
8. Ministry of Finance budget statement 2009, No. 138, at www.mofep.gov.gh/documents/budget2009.pdf, p. 35.
9. Stephanie Barrientos et al., *Mapping Sustainable Production in Ghanaian Cocoa: Report to Cadbury*, Institute of Development Studies, University of Sussex, and Department of Agricultural Economics and Agribusiness, University of Ghana, 2007, p. 10.
10. ICCO, *Quarterly Bulletin of Cocoa Statistics*, vol. 35, no. 4, Cocoa Year 2008/09.
11. Ibid.

ONE

1. Interviews took place in July/August 2007.

2. Nowell Commission Report on the Marketing of West African Cocoa, Cmnd 5845, 1938, p. 6.
3. Ibid., p. 25.
4. Ibid., p. 145.
5. Kwamina Dickson, *A Historical Geography of Ghana*, Cambridge University Press, Cambridge, 1971, p. 292.
6. Nowell Commission Report, p. 145.
7. 'Birthday of a Nation', *Time* magazine, 18 March 1957.
8. 'Ghana', *The Times*, 6 March 1957.
9. E.G. Butterworth, 'The Economy of Ghana', *Manchester Guardian*, 6 March 1957.
10. 'Birthday', *Manchester Guardian*, 6 March 1957.
11. Polly Hill, 'Cocoa Farmer', *Manchester Guardian*, 6 March 1957.
12. Dennis Austin, *Politics in Ghana, 1946–1960*, Oxford University Press, London, 1970, p. 54.
13. Ibid., p. 151; 'Death of a Deity', *Time* magazine, 8 May 1972.
14. Nowell Commission Report, p. 34.
15. Ibid., p. 162.
16. Kwame Nkrumah, *Ghana: The Autobiography of Kwame Nkrumah*, International Publishers, New York, 1970.
17. Austin, *Politics in Ghana, 1946–1960*, p. 254.
18. Ibid., p. 255.
19. Ibid., p. 267.
20. 'The New State of Ghana', *Time* magazine, 30 July 1956.
21. Cocoa Marketing Board, eighteenth annual report and accounts for period ended 28/2/1965. In 1956/57, the average sale price of cocoa was £189 per tonne; the government took £40, leaving the farmer with £149. By 1964/65, the average sale price was £171; the government took £59, leaving the farmer with £112.
22. 'Africa: On the Beach', *Time* magazine, 6 January 1967.
23. *West Africa*, 25 June 1966.
24. 'A Fateful Moment at the Maginot Hilton', *Time* magazine, 29 October 1965.
25. 'Goodbye to the Awe-ful', *Time* magazine, 4 March 1966.
26. Austin, *Politics in Ghana, 1946–1960*, p. 405.
27. 'One Party, Four Walls', *Time* magazine, 14 February 1964; 'Fruits of Redemption', *Time* magazine, 31 January 1964.
28. 'Goodbye to the Awe-ful'.
29. 'The Self-styled Redeemer Who Became a Virtual Dictator', *Manchester Guardian*, 25 February 1966.
30. Kwame Nkrumah, *Dark days in Ghana*, International Publishers, New York, 1968, p. 95.
31. 'Trouble on the Plantations', *Time* magazine, 6 August 1965.
32. 'Goodbye to the Awe-ful'.

33. 'Uprising Quelled', *Daily Graphic*, 16 May 1979; Elizabeth Ohene, *Stand Up and Be Counted: A Collection of Editorials that Redefined the June 4, 1979, Revolution in Ghana*, Blue Savannah, Accra, 2006.
34. 'Why the May 15 Uprising', *Daily Graphic*, 29 May 1979.
35. 'We Are for Total Justice', *Daily Graphic*, 6 June 1979.
36. 'Something Good out of Makola', *Daily Graphic*, 27 August 1979.
37. 'Inside the Cocoa House', *Daily Graphic*, 13 November 1979.
38. 'Rawlings: The Legacy', BBC News website, 1 December 2000.
39. Interview with former procurement agency officer, Accra, July 2007.
40. Cocobod website: www.cocobod.gh.
41. 'Ghana cut Cocobod staff from 100,000 in early 1980s to 10,000 in 1995', www.cocobod.gh/future_outlook.php.
42. http://data.un.org/CountryProfile.aspx?crName=Ghana.
43. IMF forecast for 2010.
44. I discuss in detail how Ghana rewards farmers in Chapter 7.
45. Tony Chadwick, 'Money Grows on Old Cocoa Trees', *Guardian*, 23 August 1978.
46. ICCO, *Quarterly Bulletin of Cocoa Statistics*, vol. 35, no. 4, Cocoa Year 2008/09, p. vii.
47. Stephanie Barrientos et al., *Mapping Sustainable Production in Ghanaian Cocoa: Report to Cadbury*, Institute of Development Studies, University of Sussex, and Department of Agricultural Economics and Agribusiness, University of Ghana, 2007, p. 77.

TWO

1. This is not his real name. He feared retaliation if he talked to a journalist so asked me to use a different name.
2. About 200,000 tonnes comes from Duékoué, Man, Bangolo and Guiglo and the western region. Ange Aboa, Reuters.
3. ICCO, *Quarterly Bulletin of Cocoa Statistics*, vol. 35, no. 4, Cocoa Year 2008/09, p. vii.
4. World production for 2008/09 is estimated to have been 3.5 million tonnes.
5. Cotula Lorenzo, ed., *Changes in 'Customary' Land Tenure Systems in Africa*, International Institute for Environment and Development, London, 2007, p. 75.
6. Bronwen Manby, *Struggles for Citizenship in Africa*, Zed Books, London, 2009, p. 10.
7. Kenneth B. Noble , 'Felix Houphouet-Boigny, Ivory Coast's Leader since Freedom in 1960, is Dead', *New York Times*, 8 December 1993.
8. 'Le Plan in Africa', *Time* magazine, 16 September 1966.
9. James Brooke, 'Ivory Coast: African Success Story Built on Rich Farms and Stable Politics', *New York Times*, 26 April 1988.

10. 'Juju Justice', *Time* magazine, 24 April 1964.
11. James Brooke, 'Ivory Coast Church to Tower over St Peters', *New York Times*, 19 December 1988.
12. Lyse Doucet, 'Unable to Pay', *West Africa*, 8 June 1987.
13. 'Even Côte d'Ivoire...', *West Africa*, 8 June 1987.
14. Gerald Bourke, 'Down, Down, Down', *West Africa*, 4–10 December 1989; Gerald Bourke, 'Debts and Donors, Trying to Ease the Cash Crisis', *West Africa*, 23–29 October 1989.
15. Whitney Craig, 'Jacques Foccard Dies at 83, Secret Mastermind in Africa', *New York Times,* 19 March 1997.
16. Whiteman Kaye, 'Gbagbo and Democracy', *West Africa*, 30 October 1989.
17. Manby, *Struggles for Citizenship in Africa*, p. 83.
18. Kenneth B. Noble, 'For Ivory Coast's Founder, Lavish Funeral', *New York Times*, 8 February, 1994; 'A Man of His Time', *West Africa*, 13–19 December 1993.
19. 'Black Partner', *Time* magazine, 13 February 1956.
20. Manby, *Struggles for Citizenship in Africa*, p. 32.
21. Adama Gaye, 'War over Nationality', *West Africa*, 29 November–4 December 1999.
22. 'Troops Overthrow Ivory Coast Government', *New York Times*, 25 December 1999; Karl Vick, 'Bedié Flees Ivory Coast for Togo', *Washington Post*, 27 December 1999.
23. Norimitsu Onishi, 'Dictator Gone, Violence Erupts in Ivory Coast', *New York Times*, 27 October 2000.
24. 'Mass Killing in Ivory Coast', BBC News website, 27 October 2000.
25. Onishi, 'Dictator Gone, Violence Erupts in Ivory Coast'.
26. Ibid.; 'Guei Gone', *The Economist*, 26 October 2000.
27. Stephen Smith, 'L'elu du Peuple', *Le Monde*, 26 January 2003.
28. 'A War that Threatens All the Neighbours', *The Economist*, 3 October 2002.
29. Dwayne Woods, 'The Tragedy of the Cocoa Pod: Rent-seeking, Land and Ethnic Conflict in Ivory Coast', *Journal of Modern African Studies*, vol. 41, no. 4, 2003, p. 647.
30. Manby, *Struggles for Citizenship in Africa*, p. 86.
31. 'Trapped between Two Wars: Violence against Civilians in Western Côte d'Ivoire', *Human Rights Watch Report*, August 2003, p. 45.
32. Somini Sengupta, 'Land Quarrels Unsettle Ivory Coast Cocoa Belt', *New York Times*, 26 May 2004; Lara Pawson, 'Ethnic Split Stirs Ivory Coast Crisis', BBC News website, 18 February 2004.
33. 'Trapped between Two Wars', p. 47.
34. Ibid., pp. 46, 47; 'Country on a Precipice: the Precarious State of Human Rights and Civilian Protection in Côte d'Ivoire', Human Rights Watch, 3 May 2005.

35. 'Côte d'Ivoire: What's Needed to End the Crisis', International Crisis Group, 2 July 2009.

THREE

1. Telephone interview, March 2008.
2. Raghavan Sudarsan, 'Ivory Coast Slave Traders Prey on Children's Desire to Help Their Families', Washington Bureau, 25 June 2001.
3. Raghavan Sudarsan, 'Two Teenagers Find Themselves Trapped in Slavery in Ivory Coast', Washington Bureau, 25 June 2001; Kate Blewett and Brian Woods, *Slavery: A Global Investigation*, Channel 4, 2001.
4. Blewett and Woods, *Slavery: A Global Investigation*.
5. Humphrey Hawksley, 'Mali's Children in Chocolate Slavery', BBC News website, 12 April 2001.
6. 'Summary of Findings from the Child Labour Surveys in the Cocoa Sector of West Africa: Cameroon, Côte d'Ivoire, Ghana and Nigeria', IITA, July 2002.
7. 'Third Annual Report Oversight of Public and Private Initiatives to Eliminate the Worst Forms of Child Labour in the Cocoa Sector in Côte d'Ivoire and Ghana', Payson Center for International Development and Technology Transfer, Tulane University, New Orleans, 30 September 2009. In 2006, the US Department of Labor awarded a three-year contract to the Payson Center to oversee public and private efforts to eliminate WFCL in the cocoa sector in Ghana and Côte d'Ivoire.
8. www.unicef.org/infobycountry/cotedivoire_statistics.html. A child is considered to be involved in child labour activities under the following classification: (a) children 5 to 11 years of age that during the week preceding the survey did at least one hour of economic activity or at least 28 hours of domestic work, and (b) children 12 to 14 years of age that during the week preceding the survey did at least 14 hours of economic activity or at least 42 hours of economic activity and domestic work combined.
9. www.unicef.org/infobycountry/ghana_statistics.html.
10. www.aft.org/about/world/democracy-humanrights/childlabor/cocoa.cfm.
11. Davis Lennard, 'Buying Chocolate for Valentine's Day? Think Twice!', *Huffington Post*, 6 February 2010.
12. Joanna Busza, Sarah Castle and Aisse Diarra, 'Trafficking and Health: Attempts to Prevent Trafficking Are Increasing the Problems of Those Who Migrate Voluntarily' *BMJ* 328, 5 June 2004; Sarah Castle and Aisse Diarra, 'The International Migration of Young Malians: Tradition, Necessity or Rite of Passage', London School of Hygiene and Tropical Medicine, October 2003.
13. I discuss the merits of the Fairtrade offer in detail in Chapter 6.
14. http://news.bbc.co.uk/panorama/hi/front_p./newsid_8583000/8583499.stm.

15. Exchange rate as of 13 April 2010.
16. International Cocoa Organization, *Annual Report, 2006/07*, p. 23.
17. Stephanie Barrientos, *Mapping Sustainable Production in Ghanaian Cocoa: Report to Cadbury*, Institute of Development Studies, University of Sussex, and Department of Agricultural Economics and Agribusiness, University of Ghana, 2007, p. 45.
18. Joint statement from the US Senator Tom Harkin, Representative Eliot Engel, and the Chocolate and Cocoa Industry on the implementation of the Harkin–Engel Protocol, 16 June 2008, www.worldcocoafoundation.org.
19. Ibid.
20. Information provided by Bill Guyton of the World Cocoa Foundation. The total number of farmers who have benefited from training under STCP is 97,673. This figure is cumulative since 2003 and includes farmers trained in Cameroon, Côte d'Ivoire, Ghana, Liberia and Nigeria. It includes farmers trained by other farmers and in video clubs. I focused only on those who had actually attended courses.

FOUR

1. UN Panel of Experts report, www.un.org/sc/committees/1572/CI_poe_ENG.shtmlS2005/699. In 2003, cocoa exports generated $2.3 billion, the main source of revenue for the country.
2. Interview in Paris, 19 February 2009.
3. Howard French, 'Ivory Coast Sells Itself as West African Powerhouse', *New York Times*, 9 July 1996.
4. Stephen Smith, 'Laurent Gbagbo: L'Elu du Peuple', *Le Monde*, 26 January 2004.
5. Ibid.; 'Ggagbo: Veteran Makes a Comeback', BBC News website, 27 October 2000.
6. John McIntire, principal economist World Bank, Federation of Cocoa Commerce, Response to Chairman's Speech, Cocoa Dinner, Grosvenor House, London, 7 May 1999, www.cocoafederation.com/events/speeches/1999/response.jsp.
7. Author interview.
8. Author interview with industry member.
9. Global Witness, 'Hot Chocolate: How Cocoa Fuelled the Conflict in Côte d'Ivoire', report, www.globalwitness.org, June 2007, p. 20.
10. Ibid., p. 22.
11. Ibid., p. 52.
12. Ibid.
13. Author interview in Abidjan.
14. Rory Carroll, 'Missing Reporter Stirs Trouble on Three Continents, Journalist Feared Killed for Exposing Corruption in Africa', *Observer*, 6 June 2004.

15. 'Des responsables du pouvoir ivoirien seraient liés à la disparition de Guy-André Kieffer', *Le Monde*, 26 May 2004.

16. 'Hot Chocolate', p. 24.

17. Report of the Group of Experts submitted in accordance with paragraph 9 of resolution 1643, 2005, Point 120, S/2006/735, 5 October 2006.

18. UN Panel of Experts report, www.un.org/sc/committees/1572/CI_poe_ENG.shtmlS2005/699.

19. 'Hot Chocolate', p. 51.

20. James Copnall, 'Life on Hold in Rebel-held Boauke', BBC News website, 11 May 2004.

21. Interview with Andre Ouattara, Centrale.

22. UN Panel of Experts report, Point 169, www.un.org/sc/committees/1572/CI_poe_ENG.shtmlS2009/521.

23. Ibid., Point 234.

24. 'Hot Chocolate', p. 37.

25. UN Panel of Experts report, Point 233.

26. Joan Baxter, 'Ivory Coast's Charming Rebel', BBC News website, 24 February 2003.

27. 'Hot Chocolate', pp. 33, 56; 'Pourquoi Guy André a disparu', *La Lettre du Continent*, no. 446, 29 April 2004.

28. 'Des responsables du pouvoir ivoirien seraient liés à la disparition de Guy-André Kieffer'.

29. 'Pourquoi Guy André a disparu'.

30. Carroll, 'Missing Reporter Stirs Trouble on Three Continents'.

31. Ibid.

32. 'Des responsables du pouvoir ivoirien seraient liés à la disparition de Guy-André Kieffer'; Michael Deibert, 'Côte d'Ivoire: A Call for Solidarity in Resolving Fate of Missing Reporter', Inter Press Service, 14 December 2007.

33. 'Ivory Coast First Lady Meets French Judges over Kieffer', AFP, 23 April 2009.

34. 'Un temoin relate les dernier heures du journaliste Kieffer', *Le Figaro*, 14 October 2007.

35. 'Ivory Coast First Lady Meets French Judges over Kieffer'.

36. 'Two Frenchmen Charged in Ivory Coast Kieffer Case', AFP, June 2009.

37. 'Ivory Coast Arrest Several Cocoa Officials in Corruption Crackdown', AFP, 19 June 2008.

38. 'Reviving US Chocolate Factory Proves Bittersweet', Reuters, 7 April 2006; Andrew Henderson, 'Ivory Coast Arrests Chocolate Officials', *Valley News*, 28 June 2008.

39. UN Panel of Experts report, Point 216, Point 221.

FIVE

1. Fairtrade breakdown provided by Divine Chocolate's Charlotte Berger, 28 March 2008.
2. UNIDO, *Industrial Development Report 2009: Breaking in and Moving Up: New Industrial Challenges for the Bottom Billion and Middle Income Countries*, Vienna, 2010, p. 100, Table 9.2.
3. Ibid., Manufacturing Value Added, annual growth rate by country group and region 2000–2005, Table 9.2.
4. ICCO, *Quarterly Bulletin of Cocoa Statistics*, vol. 35, no. 4, Cocoa Year 2008/09.
5. Ibid., Table 3, Estimate of production and grindings for 2008/09.
6. www.icco.org/about/processing.aspx.
7. www.nestle.com/AllAbout/History/AllHistories/1866-1905.htm.
8. www.lindtexcellence.com/about/history-of-excellence.php.
9. UNCTAD, *Cocoa Study: Industry Structures and Competition*, New York, 2008, p. 29.
10. Analyst report, *The Vontobel Food Menu: European Food & Beverage* (12 November 2007) Chocolate confectionary market: Consumption (value) by region (06), p. 19.
11. Justin Doebele, 'Chocolate Craving', *Forbes*, 9 April 2006.
12. UNCTAD, *Cocoa Study*, pp. 24, 27.
13. *The Vontobel Food Menu: European Food & Beverage* (12 November 2007), p. 22.
14. Federation of Cocoa Commerce Dinner, London, 2 June 2006.
15. UNIDO, *Industrial Development Report 2009*, p. 56, Box 5.1.
16. Ibid., p. 69.
17. Telephone interview with Food and Drink Federation, London.
18. UNIDO, *Industrial Development Report 2009*, Box 8.1.
19. UNCTAD, *Cocoa Study*, p. 31.

SIX

1. www.maketradefair.com/en/index.php?file=ghana_chris01.htm&cat=2&subcat=11&select=1, Make Trade Fair, Oxfam website.
2. http://news.bbc.co.uk/1/hi/uk_politics/1847294.stm.
3. Author interview in Kumasi, July 2007.
4. www.fairtrade.org.uk/press_office/press_releases_and_statements/archive_2002/july_2002/cocoa_prices_rise_but_farmers_stay_poor.aspx.
5. The price fixed by the government. Confirmed by FLO and Divine.
6. www.divinechocolate.com/about/story.aspx.
7. Exact market figures can vary. The figures and breakdown provided here were confirmed by two industry sources.
8. This is the figure provided by Kuapa Kokoo in Ghana. Other estimates vary. Divine suggested that Kuapa has as many as 45,000 farmers and

the Fairtrade Foundation website suggests it has as many as 50,000 farm-ers. The larger the membership, the smaller the benefits that accrue to individual farmers, so I took the smallest figure to provide the fairest, most generous representation of what Kuapa delivers to farmers on the ground.

9. Exchange rate on 17 March 2010.
10. www.cocobod.gh/news_details.php?id=47.
11. Marcella Vigneri and Paulo Santos, 'Ghana and the Cocoa Marketing Di-lemma: What Has Liberalisation without Price Competition Achieved?', *ODI Project Briefing*, December 2007.
12. 'Ghana to Raise Cocoa Producer Prices: Finmin', Reuters, 8 January 2010; conversion based on exchange rate on 17 March 2010.
13. 'Cocoa at Highest since 1970s on African Strike', *Financial Times*, 22 October 2009.
14. http://blog.worldcocoafoundation.org/2009/02/new_west_africa_cocoa_partners.php.
15. http://divinechocolateshop.com/products/divine-butterscotch-milk-chocolate-45g/.
16. Figures provided by ICCO.

SEVEN

1. ICCO, *Quarterly Bulletin of Cocoa Statistics*, vol. 35, no. 4, Cocoa year 2008/09: Table 1.
2. Paul Davis, Cocoa Dinner, Grosvenor House, London, 22 May 2009.
3. UNCTAD, *Cocoa Study: Industry Structures and Competition*, New York, 2008, p. 30.
4. Ibid., p. 29.
5. Ibid., p. 24.
6. Stephanie Barrientos et al., *Mapping Sustainable Production in Ghanaian Cocoa: Report to Cadbury*, Institute of Development Studies, University of Sussex, and Department of Agricultural Economics and Agribusiness, University of Ghana, 2007, p. 21.
7. Food and Agricultural Organization, *The State of Agricultural Com-modity Markets 2009, High Food Prices and the Food Crisis, Experiences and Lessons Learned*, Table 2, Trends in real commodity prices, Rome, p. 58.
8. Gregory Meyer, 'Academics Stand by Theory of Correlativity, *Financial Time*, 9 February 2010.
9. United States Department of Agriculture Foreign Agricultural Service FCB 2-86, October 1986, ICCO Library, London.
10. *West Africa*, 5-11 December 1988, p. 2277; James Brooke, 'Ivory Coast Gambles to Prop up Cocoa Prices', *New York Times*, 21 November, 1988.

11. Figures supplied by ICCO.
12. Figures supplied by ICCO.
13. UNCTAD, *Cocoa Study*, p. 35, Table 5: Producer prices as share of world prices; Ivorian producers received 54.27 per cent between 1990 and 1994 and 50.32 per cent between 1995 and 1999. This compares with an estimated 47.98 per cent between 2001 and 2005.
14. Matthew Green, 'Ivory Coast's Cocoa Industry Faces a Bleak Future', *Financial Times*, 15 January 2009.

EIGHT

1. J. Flood and R. Murphy (eds), *Cocoa Futures: A Source Book of Some Important Issues Facing the Cocoa Industry*, Commodities Press, Cali, Colombia, 2004, p. 42.
2. Ibid., p. 34.
3. Ibid., p. 37.
4. Ibid., p. 37.
5. ICCO, *Quarterly Bulletin of Cocoa Statistics*, vol. 35, no. 4, Cocoa year 2008/09, p. viii.
6. Just 15,500 tonnes of organic beans are grown a year. *A Study on the Market for Organic Cocoa*, EX/130/10, 26 July 2006, www.icco.org.
7. www.icco.org/about/pest.aspx.
8. Stephanie Barrientos et al., *Mapping Sustainable Production in Ghanaian Cocoa: Report to Cadbury*, Institute of Development Studies, University of Sussex, and Department of Agricultural Economics and Agribusiness, University of Ghana, 2007, p. 45.
9. Ibid.
10. ICCO, *Quarterly Bulletin of Cocoa Statistics*, vol. 35, no. 4, Cocoa year 2008/09, Table 1.
11. Ibid., p. vii.
12. Ibid., p. x.
13. Barrientos et al., *Mapping Sustainable Production in Ghanaian Cocoa*, p. 37.
14. Ibid., p. 11.
15. Bill Guyton, email interview, September 2009.
16. Alexei Kirayev, telephone interview, August 2009.
17. IMF interview, Côte d'Ivoire.
18. Peter Allum, telephone interview, August 2009.
19. ICCO, *Quarterly Bulletin of Cocoa Statistics*, vol. 35, no. 4, p. viii.
20. William Wallis, Martin Arnold and Brooke Masters, 'Corruption Probe into Sale of Ghana Oil Block', *Financial Times*, 7 January 2010.
21. Barrientos et al., *Mapping Sustainable Production in Ghanaian Cocoa*, p. 46.
22. Ibid., p. 11.

BIBLIOGRAPHY

Agyeman-Duah, Ivor (2003) *Between Faith and History: A Biography of J.A Kufuor*, Trenton NJ: Africa World Press.

Apter, David E. (1972) *Ghana in Transition*, Princeton NJ: Princeton University Press.

Austin, Dennis (1970) *Politics in Ghana 1946–1960*, Oxford: Oxford University Press.

Bales, Kevin (2000) *Disposable People: New Slavery in the Global Economy*, Berkeley: University of California Press.

Beckman, Bjorn (1976) *Organising the Farmers: Cocoa Politics and National Development in Ghana*, Uppsala: Scandinavian Institute of African Studies.

Boas, Morten, and Anne Huser (2006) 'Child Labour and Cocoa Production in West Africa: The Case of Ghana and Cote d'Ivoire', *Fafo Report 522*.

Bossard, Laurent (2003) 'Peuplement et migration en Afrique de l'Ouest: une crise régionale en Côte d'Ivoire', *Afrique contemporaine*, vol. 2, no. 206: 151–65.

Brenner, Joel Glenn (2000) *The Emperors of Chocolate: Inside the Secret World of Hershey and Mars*, New York: Broadway Books.

Chauveau, Jean-Pierre (2000) 'Question foncière et construction nationale en Côte d'Ivoire. Les enjeux silencieux d'un coup d'État', *Politique Africaine* 78.

Clarence Smith, William (1996) *Cocoa Pioneer Fronts since 1800: The Role of Smallholders, Planters and Merchants*, London: Macmillan.

Clarence Smith, William (2000) *Cocoa and Chocolate, 1765–1914*, London: Routledge.

Collier, Paul (2007) *The Bottom Billion: Why the Poorest Countries Are Failing and What Can Be Done about It*, Oxford: Oxford University Press.

Crook, Richard, et al. (2007) 'The Law, Legal Institutions and the Protection of Land Rights in Ghana and Cote d'Ivoire: Developing a More Effective and Equitable System', *IDS Research Report* 58, Brighton: IDS.

Dand, Robin (1999) *The International Cocoa Trade*, Abingdon: Woodhead.

Flood. J., and R. Murphy (eds) (2004) *Cocoa Futures: A Source Book of Some Important Issues Confronting the Cocoa Industry*, Cali, Colombia: Commodities Press.

Green R.H., and S.H. Hymer (1966) 'Cocoa in the Gold Coast: A Study in the Relations between African Farmers and Agricultural Experts', *Journal of Economic History*, vol. 26, no. 3, September: 299–319.

Hill, Polly (1998[1963]) *The Migrant Cocoa Farmers of Southern Ghana: A Study in Rural Capitalism*, Hamburg: Lit Verlag, and Oxford: James Currey for the International African Institute.

Human Rights Watch (2003) 'Trapped Between Two Wars: Violence against Civilians in Western Côte d'Ivoire', 5 August.

Human Rights Watch (2006) '"Because they have the guns ... I'm left with nothing", The Price of Continuing Impunity in Côte d'Ivoire', 25 May.

Kielland, Anne, and Maurizia Tovo (2006) *Children at Work: Child Labour Practices in Africa*, Boulder CO: Lynne Rienner.

Lieber, James (2000) *Rats in the Grain: The Dirty Tricks and Trails of Archer Daniels Midland, the Supermarket to the World*, New York: Four Walls Eight Windows.

Manby, Bronwen (2009) *Struggles for Citizenship in Africa*, London: Zed Books.

Meredith, Martin (2005) *The State of Africa: A History of 50 Years of Independence*, New York: Free Press.

Mikell, Gwendolyn (1991) *Cocoa and Chaos in Ghana*, Washington DC: Howard University Press.

Ohene, Elizabeth (2007) *Stand Up and Be Counted: A Collection of Editorials that Redefined the June 4, 1979 Revolution in Ghana*, Accra: Blue Savana.

Nkrumah, Kwame (1970) *Ghana: The Autobiography of Kwame Nkrumah*, New York: International Publishers.

Report of the Committee of Enquiry into the Existing Organisation and Methods for the Control of Swollen Shoot Disease by the Compulsory Cutting Out of Infected Cocoa Trees, Gold Coast, Accra: Government Printing Department.

Rimmer, Douglas (1984) *The Economies of West Africa*, London: Weidenfeld & Nicolson.

Rimmer, Douglas (1992) *Staying Poor: Ghana's Political Economy, 1950–1990*, Oxford: Pergamon Press.

Ruf, François, and P.S. Siswoputranto (1995) *Cocoa Cycles: The Economics of Cocoa Supply*, Abingdon: Woodhead.

Stamm, Volker (2000) *The Rural Land Plan: An Innovative Approach from Côte d'Ivoire*, International Institute for Government and Development.

Toungara, Jeanne Maddox (1990) 'The Apotheosis of Côte d'Ivoire's Nana Hou-phouët-Boigny', *Journal of Modern African Studies*, vol. 28, no. 1, March: 23-54.

Toungara, Jeanne Maddox (2001) 'Ethnicity and Political Crisis in Côte d'Ivoire', *Journal of Democracy*, vol. 12, no. 3, July: 63-72.

Woods, Dwayne (2003) 'The Tragedy of the Cocoa Pod: Rent-seeking, Land and Ethnic Conflict in Ivory Coast', *Journal of Modern African Studies*, vol. 41, no. 4, December: 641-55.

Woods, Dwayne (2004) 'Predatory Elites, Rents and Cocoa: A Comparative Analysis of Ghana and Ivory Coast', *Commonwealth & Comparative Politics*, vol. 42, no. 2, July: 224-41.

Zartman, I. William, and Christopher L. Delgado (eds) (1984) *The Political Economy of Ivory Coast*, New York: Praeger.

Zolberg, Aristide (1969) *One Party Government in the Ivory Coast*, Princeton NJ: Princeton University Press.

INDEX

AFRICAN ARGUMENTS

Written by experts with an unrivalled knowledge of the continent, African Arguments is a series of concise, engaging books that address the key issues facing Africa today. Topical and thought-provoking, accessible but in depth, they provide essential reading for anyone interested in getting to the heart of both why contemporary Africa is the way it is and how it is changing.

Series editors

Published books

Tim Allen, *Trial Justice: The International Criminal Court and the Lord's Resistance Army*
Alex de Waal, *AIDS and Power: Why There is No Political Crisis – Yet*
Raymond W. Copson, *The United States in Africa: Bush Policy and Beyond*
Chris Alden, *China in Africa*
Tom Porteous, *Britain in Africa*
Julie Flint and Alex de Waal, *Darfur: A New History of a Long War*, revised and updated edition
Jonathan Glennie, *The Trouble with Aid: Why Less Could Mean More for Africa*
Peter Uvin, *Life after Violence: A People's Story of Burundi*
Bronwen Manby, *Struggles for Citizenship in Africa*
Camilla Toulmin, *Climate Change in Africa*
Órla Ryan, *Chocolate Nations: Living and Dying for Cocoa in West Africa*

Forthcoming books

James Boyce and Leonce Ndikumana, *Africa's Odious Debts*

Mary Harper, *Getting Somalia Wrong: Faith and Hope in a Shattered State*

Theodore Trefon, *Congo Masquerade: The Political Culture of Aid Inefficiency and Reform Failure*

Gerard McCann, *India in Africa*

Tim Allen, *Trial Justice: The Lord's Resistance Army, Sudan and the International Criminal Court,* revised and updated edition

Peter da Costa, *Rethinking Africa's Institutions: The African Union, Economic Commission for Africa and African Development Bank*

Published by Zed Books and the IAI with the support of the following organisations:

InterAfrica Group   The regional centre for dialogue on development, democracy, conflict resolution and humanitarianism in the Horn of Africa. Founded in 1988 and based in Addis Ababa, with programmes supporting democracy in Ethiopia and partnership with the African Union and IGAD. www.sas.upenn.edu/African_Studies/Hornet/menu_Intr_Afr.html

International African Institute   Its principal aim is to promote scholarly understanding of Africa. Founded in 1926 and based in London, it supports a range of seminars and publications including the journal *Africa*. www. internationalafricaninstitute.org

Justice Africa   Initiates and supports African civil society activities in support of peace, justice and democracy in Africa. Founded in 1999, it has a range of activities relating to peace in the Horn of Africa, HIV/AIDS and democracy, and the African Union. www.justiceafrica.org

Royal African Society   Now more than a hundred years old, Britain's leading organisation to promote Africa's cause. Through its journal *African Affairs*, and meetings, discussions and other activities, it strengthens links between Africa and Britain. www.royalafricansociety.org

Social Science Research Council   Founded in 1923 and based in New York, it brings together researchers, practitioners and policymakers in every continent. www.ssrc.org